50
Wine Tasting
Card

WINE TASTING CARD

NAME OF WINE _____

GRAPE VARIETAL(S) _____

WHERE'S IT FROM _____

YEAR _____   WHITE / RED / ROSE (CIRCLE ONE)

LOOK

RED (SELECT ONE)

○ Purple   ○ Ruby

○ Orange   ○ Garnet

○ Brown

WHITE (SELECT ONE)

○ Straw   ○ Amber/

○ Gold   Brown

○ Yellow

IS IT FIZZY?

○ Yes   ○ No

ARE THRE ANY

PARTICLES FLOATING

IN THE GLASS?

○ A Lot

○ A Little Sediment

○ All Clear

SMELL   (Select allthat apply)

FRUIT

○ Citrus (Lemon,Lime   ○ Black (Blackberry,

  Grapefruit?)   Black Currant)

○ Tropical (Pineapple,   ○ Apple

  Melon,Lychee)   ○ Pear

○ Red (Raspberrry,   ○ Stone Fruit

  Strawberry,Cherrry)   (Peach,Apricot)

○ Blue (Blueberry)

NON-FRUIT   **OTHER**

○ Earth   ○ Vanilla   _____

○ Mushrooms   ○ Spices   _____

○ Mineral   ○ Floral   _____

○ Stone   ○ Herbs   _____

○ Oak   ○ Buttery   _____

TASTE

SWEETNESS

○ Tastes Like Candy

○ Dries Out My Mouth

○ Seem Like There's a Little Sugar

ACIDITY

○ Delightfuly Crisp

○ Like Sucking On a Lemon

○ Not Acidic

MOUTH FEEL / TANNINS

(REDS ONLY)

○ Very Smooth

○ A Little Rough Around the Edges

○ Makes Me Have to Lick My Chops

ALCOHOL

○ Not Noticeable

○ A Little Hot

○ Very Hot!

FINISH

○ Short   ○ Long

○ Medium   ○ Very Long

RATE IT !

☆ ☆ ☆ ☆ ☆

WINE TASTING CARD

NAME OF WINE _____

GRAPE VARIETAL(S) _____

WHERE'S IT FROM _____

YEAR _____ WHITE / RED / ROSE (CIRCLE ONE)

LOOK

RED (SELECT ONE)

○ Purple   ○ Ruby

○ Orange   ○ Garnet

○ Brown

WHITE (SELECT ONE)

○ Straw   ○ Amber/

○ Gold   Brown

○ Yellow

IS IT FIZZY?

○ Yes   ○ No

ARE THRE ANY

PARTICLES FLOATING

IN THE GLASS?

○ A Lot

○ A Little Sediment

○ All Clear

SMELL   (Select allthat apply)

FRUIT

○ Citrus (Lemon,Lime   ○ Black (Blackberry,

  Grapefruit?)   Black Currant)

○ Tropical (Pineapple,   ○ Apple

  Melon,Lychee)   ○ Pear

○ Red (Raspberrry,   ○ Stone Fruit

  Strawberry,Cherrry)   (Peach,Apricot)

○ Blue (Blueberry)

NON-FRUIT   **OTHER**

○ Earth   ○ Vanilla   _____

○ Mushrooms ○ Spices _____

○ Mineral ○ Floral   _____

○ Stone   ○ Herbs   _____

○ Oak   ○ Buttery   _____

TASTE

SWEETNESS

○ Tastes Like Candy

○ Dries Out My Mouth

○ Seem Like There's a Little Sugar

ACIDITY

○ Delightfuly Crisp

○ Like Sucking On a Lemon

○ Not Acidic

MOUTH FEEL / TANNINS

(REDS ONLY)

○ Very Smooth

○ A Little Rough Around the Edges

○ Makes Me Have to Lick My Chops

ALCOHOL

○ Not Noticeable

○ A Little Hot

○ Very Hot!

FINISH

○ Short   ○ Long

○ Medium   ○ Very Long

RATE IT !

☆ ☆ ☆ ☆ ☆

WINE TASTING CARD

NAME OF WINE _____

GRAPE VARIETAL(S) _____

WHERE'S IT FROM _____

YEAR _____ WHITE / RED / ROSE (CIRCLE ONE)

LOOK

RED (SELECT ONE)

- ○ Purple   ○ Ruby
- ○ Orange   ○ Garnet
- ○ Brown

WHITE (SELECT ONE)

- ○ Straw   ○ Amber/
- ○ Gold   Brown
- ○ Yellow

IS IT FIZZY?

- ○ Yes   ○ No

ARE THRE ANY PARTICLES FLOATING IN THE GLASS?

- ○ A Lot
- ○ A Little Sediment
- ○ All Clear

SMELL   (Select allthat apply)

FRUIT

- ○ Citrus (Lemon,Lime Grapefruit?)
- ○ Tropical (Pineapple, Melon,Lychee)
- ○ Red (Raspberrry, Strawberry,Cherrry)
- ○ Blue (Blueberry)
- ○ Black (Blackberry, Black Currant)
- ○ Apple
- ○ Pear
- ○ Stone Fruit (Peach,Apricot)

NON-FRUIT

- ○ Earth
- ○ Mushrooms
- ○ Mineral
- ○ Stone
- ○ Oak

- ○ Vanilla
- ○ Spices
- ○ Floral
- ○ Herbs
- ○ Buttery

OTHER

_____

_____

_____

_____

_____

TASTE

SWEETNESS

- ○ Tastes Like Candy
- ○ Dries Out My Mouth
- ○ Seem Like There's a Little Sugar

ACIDITY

- ○ Delightfuly Crisp
- ○ Like Sucking On a Lemon
- ○ Not Acidic

MOUTH FEEL / TANNINS (REDS ONLY)

- ○ Very Smooth
- ○ A Little Rough Around the Edges
- ○ Makes Me Have to Lick My Chops

ALCOHOL

- ○ Not Noticeable
- ○ A Little Hot
- ○ Very Hot!

FINISH

- ○ Short   ○ Long
- ○ Medium   ○ Very Long

RATE IT !

☆ ☆ ☆ ☆ ☆

WINE TASTING CARD

NAME OF WINE _____

GRAPE VARIETAL(S) _____

WHERE'S IT FROM _____

YEAR _____ WHITE / RED / ROSE (CIRCLE ONE)

LOOK

RED (SELECT ONE)

- ○ Purple   ○ Ruby
- ○ Orange   ○ Garnet
- ○ Brown

WHITE (SELECT ONE)

- ○ Straw   ○ Amber/
- ○ Gold   Brown
- ○ Yellow

IS IT FIZZY?

- ○ Yes   ○ No

ARE THRE ANY PARTICLES FLOATING IN THE GLASS?

- ○ A Lot
- ○ A Little Sediment
- ○ All Clear

SMELL   (Select allthat apply)

FRUIT

- ○ Citrus (Lemon,Lime Grapefruit?)
- ○ Tropical (Pineapple, Melon,Lychee)
- ○ Red (Raspberrry, Strawberry,Cherrry)
- ○ Blue (Blueberry)

- ○ Black (Blackberry, Black Currant)
- ○ Apple
- ○ Pear
- ○ Stone Fruit (Peach,Apricot)

NON-FRUIT

- ○ Earth
- ○ Mushrooms
- ○ Mineral
- ○ Stone
- ○ Oak

- ○ Vanilla
- ○ Spices
- ○ Floral
- ○ Herbs
- ○ Buttery

OTHER

- _____
- _____
- _____
- _____
- _____

TASTE

SWEETNESS

- ○ Tastes Like Candy
- ○ Dries Out My Mouth
- ○ Seem Like There's a Little Sugar

ACIDITY

- ○ Delightfuly Crisp
- ○ Like Sucking On a Lemon
- ○ Not Acidic

MOUTH FEEL / TANNINS (REDS ONLY)

- ○ Very Smooth
- ○ A Little Rough Around the Edges
- ○ Makes Me Have to Lick My Chops

ALCOHOL

- ○ Not Noticeable
- ○ A Little Hot
- ○ Very Hot!

FINISH

- ○ Short   ○ Long
- ○ Medium   ○ Very Long

RATE IT !

☆ ☆ ☆ ☆ ☆

WINE TASTING CARD

NAME OF WINE _____

GRAPE VARIETAL(S) _____

WHERE'S IT FROM _____

YEAR _____   WHITE / RED / ROSE (CIRCLE ONE)

LOOK

RED (SELECT ONE)

- ○ Purple
- ○ Ruby
- ○ Orange
- ○ Garnet
- ○ Brown

WHITE (SELECT ONE)

- ○ Straw
- ○ Amber/
- ○ Gold   Brown
- ○ Yellow

IS IT FIZZY?

- ○ Yes   ○ No

ARE THRE ANY
PARTICLES FLOATING
IN THE GLASS?

- ○ A Lot
- ○ A Little Sediment
- ○ All Clear

SMELL (Select allthat apply)

FRUIT

- ○ Citrus (Lemon,Lime Grapefruit?)
- ○ Tropical (Pineapple, Melon,Lychee)
- ○ Red (Raspberrry, Strawberry,Cherrry)
- ○ Blue (Blueberry)

- ○ Black (Blackberry, Black Currant)
- ○ Apple
- ○ Pear
- ○ Stone Fruit (Peach,Apricot)

NON-FRUIT

- ○ Earth
- ○ Mushrooms
- ○ Mineral
- ○ Stone
- ○ Oak

- ○ Vanilla
- ○ Spices
- ○ Floral
- ○ Herbs
- ○ Buttery

OTHER

_____
_____
_____
_____

TASTE

SWEETNESS

- ○ Tastes Like Candy
- ○ Dries Out My Mouth
- ○ Seem Like There's a Little Sugar

ACIDITY

- ○ Delightfuly Crisp
- ○ Like Sucking On a Lemon
- ○ Not Acidic

MOUTH FEEL / TANNINS
(REDS ONLY)

- ○ Very Smooth
- ○ A Little Rough Around the Edges
- ○ Makes Me Have to Lick My Chops

ALCOHOL

- ○ Not Noticeable
- ○ A Little Hot
- ○ Very Hot!

FINISH

- ○ Short   ○ Long
- ○ Medium   ○ Very Long

RATE IT !

☆ ☆ ☆ ☆ ☆

WINE TASTING CARD

NAME OF WINE _____

GRAPE VARIETAL(S) _____

WHERE'S IT FROM _____

YEAR _____ WHITE / RED / ROSE (CIRCLE ONE)

LOOK

RED (SELECT ONE)

- ◯ Purple   ◯ Ruby
- ◯ Orange   ◯ Garnet
- ◯ Brown

WHITE (SELECT ONE)

- ◯ Straw   ◯ Amber/
- ◯ Gold   Brown
- ◯ Yellow

IS IT FIZZY?

- ◯ Yes   ◯ No

ARE THRE ANY

PARTICLES FLOATING

IN THE GLASS?

- ◯ A Lot
- ◯ A Little Sediment
- ◯ All Clear

SMELL   (Select allthat apply)

FRUIT

- ◯ Citrus (Lemon,Lime   Grapefruit?)
- ◯ Tropical (Pineapple, Melon,Lychee)
- ◯ Red (Raspberrry, Strawberry,Cherrry)
- ◯ Blue (Blueberry)

- ◯ Black (Blackberry, Black Currant)
- ◯ Apple
- ◯ Pear
- ◯ Stone Fruit (Peach,Apricot)

NON-FRUIT

- ◯ Earth
- ◯ Mushrooms
- ◯ Mineral
- ◯ Stone
- ◯ Oak

- ◯ Vanilla
- ◯ Spices
- ◯ Floral
- ◯ Herbs
- ◯ Buttery

OTHER

_____

_____

_____

_____

_____

TASTE

SWEETNESS

- ◯ Tastes Like Candy
- ◯ Dries Out My Mouth
- ◯ Seem Like There's a Little Sugar

ACIDITY

- ◯ Delightfuly Crisp
- ◯ Like Sucking On a Lemon
- ◯ Not Acidic

MOUTH FEEL / TANNINS

(REDS ONLY)

- ◯ Very Smooth
- ◯ A Little Rough Around the Edges
- ◯ Makes Me Have to Lick My Chops

ALCOHOL

- ◯ Not Noticeable
- ◯ A Little Hot
- ◯ Very Hot!

FINISH

- ◯ Short   ◯ Long
- ◯ Medium   ◯ Very Long

RATE IT !

☆ ☆ ☆ ☆ ☆

WINE TASTING CARD

NAME OF WINE _____

GRAPE VARIETAL(S) _____

WHERE'S IT FROM _____

YEAR _____ WHITE / RED / ROSE (CIRCLE ONE)

LOOK

RED (SELECT ONE)

○ Purple ○ Ruby

○ Orange ○ Garnet

○ Brown

WHITE (SELECT ONE)

○ Straw ○ Amber/

○ Gold   Brown

○ Yellow

IS IT FIZZY?

○ Yes ○ No

ARE THRE ANY

PARTICLES FLOATING

IN THE GLASS?

○ A Lot

○ A Little Sediment

○ All Clear

SMELL (Select allthat apply)

FRUIT

○ Citrus (Lemon,Lime

  Grapefruit?)

○ Tropical (Pineapple,

  Melon,Lychee)

○ Red (Raspberrry,

  Strawberry,Cherrry)

○ Blue (Blueberry)

○ Black (Blackberry,

  Black Currant)

○ Apple

○ Pear

○ Stone Fruit

  (Peach,Apricot)

NON-FRUIT

○ Earth   ○ Vanilla

○ Mushrooms ○ Spices

○ Mineral   ○ Floral

○ Stone   ○ Herbs

○ Oak   ○ Buttery

OTHER

_____

_____

_____

_____

_____

TASTE

SWEETNESS

○ Tastes Like Candy

○ Dries Out My Mouth

○ Seem Like There's a Little Sugar

ACIDITY

○ Delightfuly Crisp

○ Like Sucking On a Lemon

○ Not Acidic

MOUTH FEEL / TANNINS

(REDS ONLY)

○ Very Smooth

○ A Little Rough Around the Edges

○ Makes Me Have to Lick My Chops

ALCOHOL

○ Not Noticeable

○ A Little Hot

○ Very Hot!

FINISH

○ Short   ○ Long

○ Medium   ○ Very Long

RATE IT !

★ ★ ★ ★ ★

WINE TASTING CARD

NAME OF WINE _____

GRAPE VARIETAL(S) _____

WHERE'S IT FROM _____

YEAR _____ WHITE / RED / ROSE (CIRCLE ONE)

LOOK

RED (SELECT ONE)

- ○ Purple   ○ Ruby
- ○ Orange   ○ Garnet
- ○ Brown

WHITE (SELECT ONE)

- ○ Straw   ○ Amber/
- ○ Gold   Brown
- ○ Yellow

IS IT FIZZY?

- ○ Yes   ○ No

ARE THRE ANY PARTICLES FLOATING IN THE GLASS?

- ○ A Lot
- ○ A Little Sediment
- ○ All Clear

SMELL   (Select allthat apply)

FRUIT

- ○ Citrus (Lemon,Lime Grapefruit?)
- ○ Tropical (Pineapple, Melon,Lychee)
- ○ Red (Raspberrry, Strawberry,Cherrry)
- ○ Blue (Blueberry)

- ○ Black (Blackberry, Black Currant)
- ○ Apple
- ○ Pear
- ○ Stone Fruit (Peach,Apricot)

NON-FRUIT

- ○ Earth
- ○ Mushrooms
- ○ Mineral
- ○ Stone
- ○ Oak

- ○ Vanilla
- ○ Spices
- ○ Floral
- ○ Herbs
- ○ Buttery

OTHER

_____

_____

_____

_____

TASTE

SWEETNESS

- ○ Tastes Like Candy
- ○ Dries Out My Mouth
- ○ Seem Like There's a Little Sugar

ACIDITY

- ○ Delightfuly Crisp
- ○ Like Sucking On a Lemon
- ○ Not Acidic

MOUTH FEEL / TANNINS (REDS ONLY)

- ○ Very Smooth
- ○ A Little Rough Around the Edges
- ○ Makes Me Have to Lick My Chops

ALCOHOL

- ○ Not Noticeable
- ○ A Little Hot
- ○ Very Hot!

FINISH

- ○ Short   ○ Long
- ○ Medium   ○ Very Long

RATE IT !

☆ ☆ ☆ ☆ ☆

WINE TASTING CARD

NAME OF WINE _____

GRAPE VARIETAL(S) _____

WHERE'S IT FROM _____

YEAR _____ WHITE / RED / ROSE (CIRCLE ONE)

LOOK

RED (SELECT ONE)

○ Purple   ○ Ruby

○ Orange   ○ Garnet

○ Brown

WHITE (SELECT ONE)

○ Straw   ○ Amber/

○ Gold   Brown

○ Yellow

IS IT FIZZY?

○ Yes   ○ No

ARE THRE ANY

PARTICLES FLOATING

IN THE GLASS?

○ A Lot

○ A Little Sediment

○ All Clear

SMELL   (Select allthat apply)

FRUIT

○ Citrus (Lemon,Lime   ○ Black (Blackberry,

    Grapefruit?)   Black Currant)

○ Tropical (Pineapple,   ○ Apple

    Melon,Lychee)   ○ Pear

○ Red (Raspberrry,   ○ Stone Fruit

    Strawberry,Cherrry)   ◡(Peach,Apricot)

○ Blue (Blueberry)

NON-FRUIT   **OTHER**

○ Earth   ○ Vanilla   _____

○ Mushrooms   ○ Spices   _____

○ Mineral   ○ Floral   _____

○ Stone   ○ Herbs   _____

○ Oak   ○ Buttery   _____

TASTE

SWEETNESS

○ Tastes Like Candy

○ Dries Out My Mouth

○ Seem Like There's a Little Sugar

ACIDITY

○ Delightfuly Crisp

○ Like Sucking On a Lemon

○ Not Acidic

MOUTH FEEL / TANNINS

(REDS ONLY)

○ Very Smooth

○ A Little Rough Around the Edges

○ Makes Me Have to Lick My Chops

ALCOHOL

○ Not Noticeable

○ A Little Hot

○ Very Hot!

FINISH

○ Short   ○ Long

○ Medium   ○ Very Long

RATE IT !

☆ ☆ ☆ ☆ ☆

WINE TASTING CARD

NAME OF WINE _____

GRAPE VARIETAL(S) _____

WHERE'S IT FROM _____

YEAR _____ WHITE / RED / ROSE (CIRCLE ONE)

LOOK

RED (SELECT ONE)

- Purple
- Ruby
- Orange
- Garnet
- Brown

WHITE (SELECT ONE)

- Straw
- Amber/
- Gold
- Brown
- Yellow

IS IT FIZZY?

- Yes
- No

ARE THRE ANY PARTICLES FLOATING IN THE GLASS?

- A Lot
- A Little Sediment
- All Clear

SMELL   (Select allthat apply)

FRUIT

- Citrus (Lemon,Lime Grapefruit?)
- Tropical (Pineapple, Melon,Lychee)
- Red (Raspberrry, Strawberry,Cherrry)
- Blue (Blueberry)
- Black (Blackberry, Black Currant)
- Apple
- Pear
- Stone Fruit (Peach,Apricot)

NON-FRUIT

- Earth
- Mushrooms
- Mineral
- Stone
- Oak
- Vanilla
- Spices
- Floral
- Herbs
- Buttery

OTHER

_____

_____

_____

_____

TASTE

SWEETNESS

- Tastes Like Candy
- Dries Out My Mouth
- Seem Like There's a Little Sugar

ACIDITY

- Delightfuly Crisp
- Like Sucking On a Lemon
- Not Acidic

MOUTH FEEL / TANNINS (REDS ONLY)

- Very Smooth
- A Little Rough Around the Edges
- Makes Me Have to Lick My Chops

ALCOHOL

- Not Noticeable
- A Little Hot
- Very Hot!

FINISH

- Short
- Long
- Medium
- Very Long

RATE IT !

☆ ☆ ☆ ☆ ☆

WINE TASTING CARD

NAME OF WINE _____

GRAPE VARIETAL(S) _____

WHERE'S IT FROM _____

YEAR _____ WHITE / RED / ROSE (CIRCLE ONE)

LOOK

RED (SELECT ONE)
- ○ Purple   ○ Ruby
- ○ Orange   ○ Garnet
- ○ Brown

WHITE (SELECT ONE)
- ○ Straw   ○ Amber/
- ○ Gold   Brown
- ○ Yellow

IS IT FIZZY?
- ○ Yes   ○ No

ARE THRE ANY PARTICLES FLOATING IN THE GLASS?
- ○ A Lot
- ○ A Little Sediment
- ○ All Clear

SMELL   (Select allthat apply)

FRUIT
- ○ Citrus (Lemon,Lime Grapefruit?)
- ○ Tropical (Pineapple, Melon,Lychee)
- ○ Red (Raspberrry, Strawberry,Cherrry)
- ○ Blue (Blueberry)
- ○ Black (Blackberry, Black Currant)
- ○ Apple
- ○ Pear
- ○ Stone Fruit (Peach,Apricot)

NON-FRUIT
- ○ Earth
- ○ Mushrooms
- ○ Mineral
- ○ Stone
- ○ Oak
- ○ Vanilla
- ○ Spices
- ○ Floral
- ○ Herbs
- ○ Buttery

OTHER
_____
_____
_____
_____

TASTE

SWEETNESS
- ○ Tastes Like Candy
- ○ Dries Out My Mouth
- ○ Seem Like There's a Little Sugar

ACIDITY
- ○ Delightfuly Crisp
- ○ Like Sucking On a Lemon
- ○ Not Acidic

MOUTH FEEL / TANNINS (REDS ONLY)
- ○ Very Smooth
- ○ A Little Rough Around the Edges
- ○ Makes Me Have to Lick My Chops

ALCOHOL
- ○ Not Noticeable
- ○ A Little Hot
- ○ Very Hot!

FINISH
- ○ Short   ○ Long
- ○ Medium   ○ Very Long

RATE IT !

☆ ☆ ☆ ☆ ☆

WINE TASTING CARD

NAME OF WINE _____

GRAPE VARIETAL(S) _____

WHERE'S IT FROM _____

YEAR _____ WHITE / RED / ROSE (CIRCLE ONE)

LOOK

RED (SELECT ONE)

○ Purple ○ Ruby

○ Orange ○ Garnet

○ Brown

WHITE (SELECT ONE)

○ Straw ○ Amber/

○ Gold   Brown

○ Yellow

IS IT FIZZY?

○ Yes ○ No

ARE THRE ANY

PARTICLES FLOATING

IN THE GLASS?

○ A Lot

○ A Little Sediment

○ All Clear

SMELL (Select allthat apply)

FRUIT

○ Citrus (Lemon,Lime   ○ Black (Blackberry,
   Grapefruit?)   Black Currant)

○ Tropical (Pineapple,   ○ Apple
   Melon,Lychee)

○ Red (Raspberrry,   ○ Pear
   Strawberry,Cherrry)

                              ○ Stone Fruit
                                 (Peach,Apricot)

○ Blue (Blueberry)

NON-FRUIT   **OTHER**

○ Earth   ○ Vanilla   _____

○ Mushrooms ○ Spices   _____

○ Mineral   ○ Floral   _____

○ Stone   ○ Herbs   _____

○ Oak   ○ Buttery   _____

TASTE

SWEETNESS

○ Tastes Like Candy

○ Dries Out My Mouth

○ Seem Like There's a Little Sugar

ACIDITY

○ Delightfuly Crisp

○ Like Sucking On a Lemon

○ Not Acidic

MOUTH FEEL / TANNINS

(REDS ONLY)

○ Very Smooth

○ A Little Rough Around the Edges

○ Makes Me Have to Lick My Chops

ALCOHOL

○ Not Noticeable

○ A Little Hot

○ Very Hot!

FINISH

○ Short   ○ Long

○ Medium   ○ Very Long

RATE IT !

☆ ☆ ☆ ☆ ☆

WINE TASTING CARD

NAME OF WINE _____

GRAPE VARIETAL(S) _____

WHERE'S IT FROM _____

YEAR _____ WHITE / RED / ROSE (CIRCLE ONE)

LOOK

RED (SELECT ONE)
- ○ Purple ○ Ruby
- ○ Orange ○ Garnet
- ○ Brown

WHITE (SELECT ONE)
- ○ Straw ○ Amber/
- ○ Gold   Brown
- ○ Yellow

IS IT FIZZY?
- ○ Yes ○ No

ARE THRE ANY PARTICLES FLOATING IN THE GLASS?
- ○ A Lot
- ○ A Little Sediment
- ○ All Clear

SMELL (Select allthat apply)

FRUIT
- ○ Citrus (Lemon,Lime Grapefruit?)
- ○ Tropical (Pineapple, Melon,Lychee)
- ○ Red (Raspberrry, Strawberry,Cherrry)
- ○ Blue (Blueberry)

- ○ Black (Blackberry, Black Currant)
- ○ Apple
- ○ Pear
- ○ Stone Fruit (Peach,Apricot)

NON-FRUIT
- ○ Earth
- ○ Mushrooms
- ○ Mineral
- ○ Stone
- ○ Oak

- ○ Vanilla
- ○ Spices
- ○ Floral
- ○ Herbs
- ○ Buttery

OTHER
_____
_____
_____
_____

TASTE

SWEETNESS
- ○ Tastes Like Candy
- ○ Dries Out My Mouth
- ○ Seem Like There's a Little Sugar

ACIDITY
- ○ Delightfuly Crisp
- ○ Like Sucking On a Lemon
- ○ Not Acidic

MOUTH FEEL / TANNINS (REDS ONLY)
- ○ Very Smooth
- ○ A Little Rough Around the Edges
- ○ Makes Me Have to Lick My Chops

ALCOHOL
- ○ Not Noticeable
- ○ A Little Hot
- ○ Very Hot!

FINISH
- ○ Short ○ Long
- ○ Medium ○ Very Long

RATE IT !

☆ ☆ ☆ ☆ ☆

WINE TASTING CARD

NAME OF WINE _____

GRAPE VARIETAL(S) _____

WHERE'S IT FROM _____

YEAR _____ WHITE / RED / ROSE (CIRCLE ONE)

LOOK

RED (SELECT ONE)

- ○ Purple   ○ Ruby
- ○ Orange   ○ Garnet
- ○ Brown

WHITE (SELECT ONE)

- ○ Straw   ○ Amber/
- ○ Gold   Brown
- ○ Yellow

IS IT FIZZY?

- ○ Yes   ○ No

ARE THRE ANY PARTICLES FLOATING IN THE GLASS?

- ○ A Lot
- ○ A Little Sediment
- ○ All Clear

SMELL   (Select allthat apply)

FRUIT

- ○ Citrus (Lemon,Lime Grapefruit?)
- ○ Tropical (Pineapple, Melon,Lychee)
- ○ Red (Raspberrry, Strawberry,Cherrry)
- ○ Blue (Blueberry)

- ○ Black (Blackberry, Black Currant)
- ○ Apple
- ○ Pear
- ○ Stone Fruit (Peach,Apricot)

NON-FRUIT

- ○ Earth
- ○ Mushrooms
- ○ Mineral
- ○ Stone
- ○ Oak

- ○ Vanilla
- ○ Spices
- ○ Floral
- ○ Herbs
- ○ Buttery

OTHER

- _____
- _____
- _____
- _____
- _____

TASTE

SWEETNESS

- ○ Tastes Like Candy
- ○ Dries Out My Mouth
- ○ Seem Like There's a Little Sugar

ACIDITY

- ○ Delightfuly Crisp
- ○ Like Sucking On a Lemon
- ○ Not Acidic

MOUTH FEEL / TANNINS (REDS ONLY)

- ○ Very Smooth
- ○ A Little Rough Around the Edges
- ○ Makes Me Have to Lick My Chops

ALCOHOL

- ○ Not Noticeable
- ○ A Little Hot
- ○ Very Hot!

FINISH

- ○ Short   ○ Long
- ○ Medium   ○ Very Long

RATE IT !

★ ★ ★ ★ ★

WINE TASTING CARD

NAME OF WINE _____

GRAPE VARIETAL(S) _____

WHERE'S IT FROM _____

YEAR _____ WHITE / RED / ROSE (CIRCLE ONE)

LOOK

RED (SELECT ONE)

- Purple
- Ruby
- Orange
- Garnet
- Brown

WHITE (SELECT ONE)

- Straw
- Amber/
- Gold
  Brown
- Yellow

IS IT FIZZY?

- Yes
- No

ARE THRE ANY

PARTICLES FLOATING

IN THE GLASS?

- A Lot
- A Little Sediment
- All Clear

SMELL (Select allthat apply)

FRUIT

- Citrus (Lemon,Lime Grapefruit?)
- Tropical (Pineapple, Melon,Lychee)
- Red (Raspberrry, Strawberry,Cherrry)
- Blue (Blueberry)
- Black (Blackberry, Black Currant)
- Apple
- Pear
- Stone Fruit (Peach,Apricot)

NON-FRUIT

- Earth
- Mushrooms
- Mineral
- Stone
- Oak
- Vanilla
- Spices
- Floral
- Herbs
- Buttery

OTHER

_____

_____

_____

_____

TASTE

SWEETNESS

- Tastes Like Candy
- Dries Out My Mouth
- Seem Like There's a Little Sugar

ACIDITY

- Delightfuly Crisp
- Like Sucking On a Lemon
- Not Acidic

MOUTH FEEL / TANNINS

(REDS ONLY)

- Very Smooth
- A Little Rough Around the Edges
- Makes Me Have to Lick My Chops

ALCOHOL

- Not Noticeable
- A Little Hot
- Very Hot!

FINISH

- Short
- Long
- Medium
- Very Long

RATE IT !

☆ ☆ ☆ ☆ ☆

WINE TASTING CARD

NAME OF WINE _____

GRAPE VARIETAL(S) _____

WHERE'S IT FROM _____

YEAR _____   WHITE / RED / ROSE (CIRCLE ONE)

LOOK

RED (SELECT ONE)

- ○ Purple   ○ Ruby
- ○ Orange   ○ Garnet
- ○ Brown

WHITE (SELECT ONE)

- ○ Straw   ○ Amber/
- ○ Gold   Brown
- ○ Yellow

IS IT FIZZY?

- ○ Yes   ○ No

ARE THRE ANY

PARTICLES FLOATING

IN THE GLASS?

- ○ A Lot
- ○ A Little Sediment
- ○ All Clear

SMELL   (Select allthat apply)

FRUIT

- ○ Citrus (Lemon,Lime Grapefruit?)
- ○ Tropical (Pineapple, Melon,Lychee)
- ○ Red (Raspberrry, Strawberry,Cherrry)
- ○ Blue (Blueberry)

- ○ Black (Blackberry, Black Currant)
- ○ Apple
- ○ Pear
- ○ Stone Fruit (Peach,Apricot)

NON-FRUIT

- ○ Earth
- ○ Mushrooms
- ○ Mineral
- ○ Stone
- ○ Oak

- ○ Vanilla
- ○ Spices
- ○ Floral
- ○ Herbs
- ○ Buttery

OTHER

_____

_____

_____

_____

_____

TASTE

SWEETNESS

- ○ Tastes Like Candy
- ○ Dries Out My Mouth
- ○ Seem Like There's a Little Sugar

ACIDITY

- ○ Delightfuly Crisp
- ○ Like Sucking On a Lemon
- ○ Not Acidic

MOUTH FEEL / TANNINS (REDS ONLY)

- ○ Very Smooth
- ○ A Little Rough Around the Edges
- ○ Makes Me Have to Lick My Chops

ALCOHOL

- ○ Not Noticeable
- ○ A Little Hot
- ○ Very Hot!

FINISH

- ○ Short   ○ Long
- ○ Medium   ○ Very Long

RATE IT !

★ ★ ★ ★ ★

WINE TASTING CARD

NAME OF WINE _____

GRAPE VARIETAL(S) _____

WHERE'S IT FROM _____

YEAR _____ WHITE / RED / ROSE (CIRCLE ONE)

LOOK

RED (SELECT ONE)

- ○ Purple
- ○ Ruby
- ○ Orange
- ○ Garnet
- ○ Brown

WHITE (SELECT ONE)

- ○ Straw
- ○ Amber/
- ○ Gold   Brown
- ○ Yellow

IS IT FIZZY?

- ○ Yes
- ○ No

ARE THRE ANY PARTICLES FLOATING IN THE GLASS?

- ○ A Lot
- ○ A Little Sediment
- ○ All Clear

SMELL   (Select all that apply)

FRUIT

- ○ Citrus (Lemon, Lime Grapefruit?)
- ○ Tropical (Pineapple, Melon, Lychee)
- ○ Red (Raspberrry, Strawberry, Cherrry)
- ○ Blue (Blueberry)

- ○ Black (Blackberry, Black Currant)
- ○ Apple
- ○ Pear
- ○ Stone Fruit (Peach, Apricot)

NON-FRUIT

- ○ Earth
- ○ Mushrooms
- ○ Mineral
- ○ Stone
- ○ Oak

- ○ Vanilla
- ○ Spices
- ○ Floral
- ○ Herbs
- ○ Buttery

OTHER

_____

_____

_____

_____

_____

TASTE

SWEETNESS

- ○ Tastes Like Candy
- ○ Dries Out My Mouth
- ○ Seem Like There's a Little Sugar

ACIDITY

- ○ Delightfuly Crisp
- ○ Like Sucking On a Lemon
- ○ Not Acidic

MOUTH FEEL / TANNINS (REDS ONLY)

- ○ Very Smooth
- ○ A Little Rough Around the Edges
- ○ Makes Me Have to Lick My Chops

ALCOHOL

- ○ Not Noticeable
- ○ A Little Hot
- ○ Very Hot!

FINISH

- ○ Short
- ○ Medium
- ○ Long
- ○ Very Long

RATE IT !

☆ ☆ ☆ ☆ ☆

WINE TASTING CARD

NAME OF WINE _____

GRAPE VARIETAL(S) _____

WHERE'S IT FROM _____

YEAR _____ WHITE / RED / ROSE (CIRCLE ONE)

LOOK

RED (SELECT ONE)

○ Purple ○ Ruby

○ Orange ○ Garnet

○ Brown

WHITE (SELECT ONE)

○ Straw ○ Amber/

○ Gold   Brown

○ Yellow

IS IT FIZZY?

○ Yes ○ No

ARE THRE ANY

PARTICLES FLOATING

IN THE GLASS?

○ A Lot

○ A Little Sediment

○ All Clear

SMELL   (Select allthat apply)

FRUIT

○ Citrus (Lemon,Lime   ○ Black (Blackberry,

   Grapefruit?)   Black Currant)

○ Tropical (Pineapple,   ○ Apple

   Melon,Lychee)   ○ Pear

○ Red (Raspberrry,   ○ Stone Fruit

   Strawberry,Cherrry)   (Peach,Apricot)

○ Blue (Blueberry)

NON-FRUIT   **OTHER**

○ Earth   ○ Vanilla   _____

○ Mushrooms   ○ Spices   _____

○ Mineral   ○ Floral   _____

○ Stone   ○ Herbs   _____

○ Oak   ○ Buttery   _____

TASTE

SWEETNESS

○ Tastes Like Candy

○ Dries Out My Mouth

○ Seem Like There's a Little Sugar

ACIDITY

○ Delightfuly Crisp

○ Like Sucking On a Lemon

○ Not Acidic

MOUTH FEEL / TANNINS

(REDS ONLY)

○ Very Smooth

○ A Little Rough Around the Edges

○ Makes Me Have to Lick My Chops

ALCOHOL

○ Not Noticeable

○ A Little Hot

○ Very Hot!

FINISH

○ Short   ○ Long

○ Medium   ○ Very Long

RATE IT !

☆ ☆ ☆ ☆ ☆

WINE TASTING CARD

NAME OF WINE _____

GRAPE VARIETAL(S) _____

WHERE'S IT FROM _____

YEAR _____ WHITE / RED / ROSE (CIRCLE ONE)

LOOK

RED (SELECT ONE)

- ○ Purple   ○ Ruby
- ○ Orange   ○ Garnet
- ○ Brown

WHITE (SELECT ONE)

- ○ Straw   ○ Amber/
- ○ Gold   Brown
- ○ Yellow

IS IT FIZZY?

- ○ Yes   ○ No

ARE THRE ANY PARTICLES FLOATING IN THE GLASS?

- ○ A Lot
- ○ A Little Sediment
- ○ All Clear

SMELL   (Select allthat apply)

FRUIT

- ○ Citrus (Lemon,Lime Grapefruit?)
- ○ Tropical (Pineapple, Melon,Lychee)
- ○ Red (Raspberrry, Strawberry,Cherrry)
- ○ Blue (Blueberry)

- ○ Black (Blackberry, Black Currant)
- ○ Apple
- ○ Pear
- ○ Stone Fruit (Peach,Apricot)

NON-FRUIT

- ○ Earth
- ○ Mushrooms
- ○ Mineral
- ○ Stone
- ○ Oak

- ○ Vanilla
- ○ Spices
- ○ Floral
- ○ Herbs
- ○ Buttery

OTHER

_____

_____

_____

_____

_____

TASTE

SWEETNESS

- ○ Tastes Like Candy
- ○ Dries Out My Mouth
- ○ Seem Like There's a Little Sugar

ACIDITY

- ○ Delightfuly Crisp
- ○ Like Sucking On a Lemon
- ○ Not Acidic

MOUTH FEEL / TANNINS (REDS ONLY)

- ○ Very Smooth
- ○ A Little Rough Around the Edges
- ○ Makes Me Have to Lick My Chops

ALCOHOL

- ○ Not Noticeable
- ○ A Little Hot
- ○ Very Hot!

FINISH

- ○ Short   ○ Long
- ○ Medium   ○ Very Long

RATE IT !

☆ ☆ ☆ ☆ ☆

WINE TASTING CARD

NAME OF WINE _____

GRAPE VARIETAL(S) _____

WHERE'S IT FROM _____

YEAR _____ WHITE / RED / ROSE (CIRCLE ONE)

LOOK

RED (SELECT ONE)

○ Purple   ○ Ruby

○ Orange   ○ Garnet

○ Brown

WHITE (SELECT ONE)

○ Straw   ○ Amber/

○ Gold   Brown

○ Yellow

IS IT FIZZY?

○ Yes   ○ No

ARE THRE ANY

PARTICLES FLOATING

IN THE GLASS?

○ A Lot

○ A Little Sediment

○ All Clear

SMELL (Select allthat apply)

FRUIT

○ Citrus (Lemon,Lime   ○ Black (Blackberry,

   Grapefruit?)   Black Currant)

○ Tropical (Pineapple,   ○ Apple

   Melon,Lychee)   ○ Pear

○ Red (Raspberrry,   ○ Stone Fruit

   Strawberry,Cherrry)   (Peach,Apricot)

○ Blue (Blueberry)

NON-FRUIT   **OTHER**

○ Earth   ○ Vanilla   _____

○ Mushrooms ○ Spices   _____

○ Mineral   ○ Floral   _____

○ Stone   ○ Herbs   _____

○ Oak   ○ Buttery   _____

TASTE

SWEETNESS

○ Tastes Like Candy

○ Dries Out My Mouth

○ Seem Like There's a Little Sugar

ACIDITY

○ Delightfuly Crisp

○ Like Sucking On a Lemon

○ Not Acidic

MOUTH FEEL / TANNINS

(REDS ONLY)

○ Very Smooth

○ A Little Rough Around the Edges

○ Makes Me Have to Lick My Chops

ALCOHOL

○ Not Noticeable

○ A Little Hot

○ Very Hot!

FINISH

○ Short   ○ Long

○ Medium   ○ Very Long

RATE IT !

⭐ ⭐ ⭐ ⭐ ⭐

WINE TASTING CARD

NAME OF WINE _____

GRAPE VARIETAL(S) _____

WHERE'S IT FROM _____

YEAR _____ WHITE / RED / ROSE (CIRCLE ONE)

LOOK

RED (SELECT ONE)

○ Purple   ○ Ruby

○ Orange   ○ Garnet

○ Brown

WHITE (SELECT ONE)

○ Straw   ○ Amber/

○ Gold   Brown

○ Yellow

IS IT FIZZY?

○ Yes   ○ No

ARE THRE ANY

PARTICLES FLOATING

IN THE GLASS?

○ A Lot

○ A Little Sediment

○ All Clear

SMELL   (Select allthat apply)

FRUIT

○ Citrus (Lemon,Lime
  Grapefruit?)

○ Tropical (Pineapple,
  Melon,Lychee)

○ Red (Raspberrry,
  Strawberry,Cherrry)

○ Blue (Blueberry)

○ Black (Blackberry,
  Black Currant)

○ Apple

○ Pear

○ Stone Fruit
  (Peach,Apricot)

NON-FRUIT

○ Earth   ○ Vanilla

○ Mushrooms   ○ Spices

○ Mineral   ○ Floral

○ Stone   ○ Herbs

○ Oak   ○ Buttery

OTHER

_____

_____

_____

_____

TASTE

SWEETNESS

○ Tastes Like Candy

○ Dries Out My Mouth

○ Seem Like There's a Little Sugar

ACIDITY

○ Delightfuly Crisp

○ Like Sucking On a Lemon

○ Not Acidic

MOUTH FEEL / TANNINS

(REDS ONLY)

○ Very Smooth

○ A Little Rough Around the Edges

○ Makes Me Have to Lick My Chops

ALCOHOL

○ Not Noticeable

○ A Little Hot

○ Very Hot!

FINISH

○ Short   ○ Long

○ Medium   ○ Very Long

RATE IT !

☆ ☆ ☆ ☆ ☆

WINE TASTING CARD

NAME OF WINE _____

GRAPE VARIETAL(S) _____

WHERE'S IT FROM _____

YEAR _____ WHITE / RED / ROSE (CIRCLE ONE)

LOOK

RED (SELECT ONE)

- ○ Purple   ○ Ruby
- ○ Orange   ○ Garnet
- ○ Brown

WHITE (SELECT ONE)

- ○ Straw   ○ Amber/
- ○ Gold   Brown
- ○ Yellow

IS IT FIZZY?

- ○ Yes   ○ No

ARE THRE ANY

PARTICLES FLOATING

IN THE GLASS?

- ○ A Lot
- ○ A Little Sediment
- ○ All Clear

SMELL   (Select allthat apply)

FRUIT

- ○ Citrus (Lemon, Lime Grapefruit?)
- ○ Tropical (Pineapple, Melon, Lychee)
- ○ Red (Raspberrry, Strawberry, Cherrry)
- ○ Blue (Blueberry)

- ○ Black (Blackberry, Black Currant)
- ○ Apple
- ○ Pear
- ○ Stone Fruit (Peach, Apricot)

NON-FRUIT

- ○ Earth   ○ Vanilla
- ○ Mushrooms   ○ Spices
- ○ Mineral   ○ Floral
- ○ Stone   ○ Herbs
- ○ Oak   ○ Buttery

OTHER

_____

_____

_____

_____

_____

TASTE

SWEETNESS

- ○ Tastes Like Candy
- ○ Dries Out My Mouth
- ○ Seem Like There's a Little Sugar

ACIDITY

- ○ Delightfuly Crisp
- ○ Like Sucking On a Lemon
- ○ Not Acidic

MOUTH FEEL / TANNINS

(REDS ONLY)

- ○ Very Smooth
- ○ A Little Rough Around the Edges
- ○ Makes Me Have to Lick My Chops

ALCOHOL

- ○ Not Noticeable
- ○ A Little Hot
- ○ Very Hot!

FINISH

- ○ Short   ○ Long
- ○ Medium   ○ Very Long

RATE IT !

☆ ☆ ☆ ☆ ☆

WINE TASTING CARD

NAME OF WINE _____

GRAPE VARIETAL(S) _____

WHERE'S IT FROM _____

YEAR _____ WHITE / RED / ROSE (CIRCLE ONE)

LOOK

RED (SELECT ONE)

- ○ Purple   ○ Ruby
- ○ Orange   ○ Garnet
- ○ Brown

WHITE (SELECT ONE)

- ○ Straw   ○ Amber/
- ○ Gold   Brown
- ○ Yellow

IS IT FIZZY?

- ○ Yes   ○ No

ARE THRE ANY PARTICLES FLOATING IN THE GLASS?

- ○ A Lot
- ○ A Little Sediment
- ○ All Clear

SMELL (Select allthat apply)

FRUIT

- ○ Citrus (Lemon,Lime Grapefruit?)
- ○ Tropical (Pineapple, Melon,Lychee)
- ○ Red (Raspberrry, Strawberry,Cherrry)
- ○ Blue (Blueberry)

- ○ Black (Blackberry, Black Currant)
- ○ Apple
- ○ Pear
- ○ Stone Fruit (Peach,Apricot)

NON-FRUIT

- ○ Earth
- ○ Mushrooms
- ○ Mineral
- ○ Stone
- ○ Oak

- ○ Vanilla
- ○ Spices
- ○ Floral
- ○ Herbs
- ○ Buttery

OTHER

- _____
- _____
- _____
- _____
- _____

TASTE

SWEETNESS

- ○ Tastes Like Candy
- ○ Dries Out My Mouth
- ○ Seem Like There's a Little Sugar

ACIDITY

- ○ Delightfuly Crisp
- ○ Like Sucking On a Lemon
- ○ Not Acidic

MOUTH FEEL / TANNINS (REDS ONLY)

- ○ Very Smooth
- ○ A Little Rough Around the Edges
- ○ Makes Me Have to Lick My Chops

ALCOHOL

- ○ Not Noticeable
- ○ A Little Hot
- ○ Very Hot!

FINISH

- ○ Short   ○ Long
- ○ Medium   ○ Very Long

RATE IT !

☆ ☆ ☆ ☆ ☆

WINE TASTING CARD

NAME OF WINE _____

GRAPE VARIETAL(S) _____

WHERE'S IT FROM _____

YEAR _____ WHITE / RED / ROSE (CIRCLE ONE)

LOOK

RED (SELECT ONE)
- ○ Purple   ○ Ruby
- ○ Orange   ○ Garnet
- ○ Brown

WHITE (SELECT ONE)
- ○ Straw   ○ Amber/
- ○ Gold   Brown
- ○ Yellow

IS IT FIZZY?
- ○ Yes   ○ No

ARE THRE ANY PARTICLES FLOATING IN THE GLASS?
- ○ A Lot
- ○ A Little Sediment
- ○ All Clear

SMELL (Select allthat apply)

FRUIT
- ○ Citrus (Lemon,Lime Grapefruit?)
- ○ Tropical (Pineapple, Melon,Lychee)
- ○ Red (Raspberrry, Strawberry,Cherrry)
- ○ Blue (Blueberry)
- ○ Black (Blackberry, Black Currant)
- ○ Apple
- ○ Pear
- ○ Stone Fruit (Peach,Apricot)

NON-FRUIT
- ○ Earth   ○ Vanilla
- ○ Mushrooms   ○ Spices
- ○ Mineral   ○ Floral
- ○ Stone   ○ Herbs
- ○ Oak   ○ Buttery

OTHER
- _____
- _____
- _____
- _____
- _____

TASTE

SWEETNESS
- ○ Tastes Like Candy
- ○ Dries Out My Mouth
- ○ Seem Like There's a Little Sugar

ACIDITY
- ○ Delightfuly Crisp
- ○ Like Sucking On a Lemon
- ○ Not Acidic

MOUTH FEEL / TANNINS (REDS ONLY)
- ○ Very Smooth
- ○ A Little Rough Around the Edges
- ○ Makes Me Have to Lick My Chops

ALCOHOL
- ○ Not Noticeable
- ○ A Little Hot
- ○ Very Hot!

FINISH
- ○ Short   ○ Long
- ○ Medium   ○ Very Long

RATE IT !

☆ ☆ ☆ ☆ ☆

WINE TASTING CARD

NAME OF WINE _____

GRAPE VARIETAL(S) _____

WHERE'S IT FROM _____

YEAR _____ WHITE / RED / ROSE (CIRCLE ONE)

LOOK

RED (SELECT ONE)

○ Purple   ○ Ruby

○ Orange   ○ Garnet

○ Brown

WHITE (SELECT ONE)

○ Straw   ○ Amber/

○ Gold   Brown

○ Yellow

IS IT FIZZY?

○ Yes   ○ No

ARE THRE ANY

PARTICLES FLOATING

IN THE GLASS?

○ A Lot

○ A Little Sediment

○ All Clear

SMELL   (Select allthat apply)

FRUIT

○ Citrus (Lemon,Lime   ○ Black (Blackberry,

   Grapefruit?)   Black Currant)

○ Tropical (Pineapple,   ○ Apple

   Melon,Lychee)   ○ Pear

○ Red (Raspberrry,   ○ Stone Fruit

   Strawberry,Cherrry)   (Peach,Apricot)

○ Blue (Blueberry)

NON-FRUIT   **OTHER**

○ Earth   ○ Vanilla   _____

○ Mushrooms   ○ Spices   _____

○ Mineral   ○ Floral   _____

○ Stone   ○ Herbs   _____

○ Oak   ○ Buttery   _____

TASTE

SWEETNESS

○ Tastes Like Candy

○ Dries Out My Mouth

○ Seem Like There's a Little Sugar

ACIDITY

○ Delightfuly Crisp

○ Like Sucking On a Lemon

○ Not Acidic

MOUTH FEEL / TANNINS

(REDS ONLY)

○ Very Smooth

○ A Little Rough Around the Edges

○ Makes Me Have to Lick My Chops

ALCOHOL

○ Not Noticeable

○ A Little Hot

○ Very Hot!

FINISH

○ Short   ○ Long

○ Medium   ○ Very Long

RATE IT !

☆ ☆ ☆ ☆ ☆

WINE TASTING CARD

NAME OF WINE _____

GRAPE VARIETAL(S) _____

WHERE'S IT FROM _____

YEAR _____ WHITE / RED / ROSE (CIRCLE ONE)

LOOK

RED (SELECT ONE)

○ Purple   ○ Ruby

○ Orange   ○ Garnet

○ Brown

WHITE (SELECT ONE)

○ Straw   ○ Amber/

○ Gold   Brown

○ Yellow

IS IT FIZZY?

○ Yes   ○ No

ARE THRE ANY

PARTICLES FLOATING

IN THE GLASS?

○ A Lot

○ A Little Sediment

○ All Clear

SMELL (Select allthat apply)

FRUIT

○ Citrus (Lemon,Lime   ○ Black (Blackberry,

　Grapefruit?)   　Black Currant)

○ Tropical (Pineapple,   ○ Apple

　Melon,Lychee)   ○ Pear

○ Red (Raspberrry,   ○ Stone Fruit

　Strawberry,Cherrry)   　(Peach,Apricot)

○ Blue (Blueberry)

NON-FRUIT   **OTHER**

○ Earth   ○ Vanilla   _____

○ Mushrooms   ○ Spices   _____

○ Mineral   ○ Floral   _____

○ Stone   ○ Herbs   _____

○ Oak   ○ Buttery   _____

TASTE

SWEETNESS

○ Tastes Like Candy

○ Dries Out My Mouth

○ Seem Like There's a Little Sugar

ACIDITY

○ Delightfuly Crisp

○ Like Sucking On a Lemon

○ Not Acidic

MOUTH FEEL / TANNINS

(REDS ONLY)

○ Very Smooth

○ A Little Rough Around the Edges

○ Makes Me Have to Lick My Chops

ALCOHOL

○ Not Noticeable

○ A Little Hot

○ Very Hot!

FINISH

○ Short   ○ Long

○ Medium   ○ Very Long

RATE IT !

☆ ☆ ☆ ☆ ☆

WINE TASTING CARD

NAME OF WINE _____

GRAPE VARIETAL(S) _____

WHERE'S IT FROM _____

YEAR _____ WHITE / RED / ROSE (CIRCLE ONE)

LOOK

RED (SELECT ONE)

- ○ Purple   ○ Ruby
- ○ Orange   ○ Garnet
- ○ Brown

WHITE (SELECT ONE)

- ○ Straw   ○ Amber/
- ○ Gold   Brown
- ○ Yellow

IS IT FIZZY?

- ○ Yes   ○ No

ARE THRE ANY
PARTICLES FLOATING
IN THE GLASS?

- ○ A Lot
- ○ A Little Sediment
- ○ All Clear

SMELL   (Select allthat apply)

FRUIT

- ○ Citrus (Lemon,Lime Grapefruit?)
- ○ Tropical (Pineapple, Melon,Lychee)
- ○ Red (Raspberrry, Strawberry,Cherrry)
- ○ Blue (Blueberry)
- ○ Black (Blackberry, Black Currant)
- ○ Apple
- ○ Pear
- ○ Stone Fruit (Peach,Apricot)

NON-FRUIT

- ○ Earth
- ○ Mushrooms
- ○ Mineral
- ○ Stone
- ○ Oak
- ○ Vanilla
- ○ Spices
- ○ Floral
- ○ Herbs
- ○ Buttery

OTHER

_____
_____
_____
_____
_____

TASTE

SWEETNESS

- ○ Tastes Like Candy
- ○ Dries Out My Mouth
- ○ Seem Like There's a Little Sugar

ACIDITY

- ○ Delightfuly Crisp
- ○ Like Sucking On a Lemon
- ○ Not Acidic

MOUTH FEEL / TANNINS
(REDS ONLY)

- ○ Very Smooth
- ○ A Little Rough Around the Edges
- ○ Makes Me Have to Lick My Chops

ALCOHOL

- ○ Not Noticeable
- ○ A Little Hot
- ○ Very Hot!

FINISH

- ○ Short   ○ Long
- ○ Medium   ○ Very Long

RATE IT !

☆ ☆ ☆ ☆ ☆

WINE TASTING CARD

NAME OF WINE _____

GRAPE VARIETAL(S) _____

WHERE'S IT FROM _____

YEAR _____ WHITE / RED / ROSE (CIRCLE ONE)

LOOK

RED (SELECT ONE)

○ Purple   ○ Ruby

○ Orange   ○ Garnet

○ Brown

WHITE (SELECT ONE)

○ Straw   ○ Amber/

○ Gold   Brown

○ Yellow

IS IT FIZZY?

○ Yes   ○ No

ARE THRE ANY
PARTICLES FLOATING
IN THE GLASS?

○ A Lot

○ A Little Sediment

○ All Clear

SMELL   (Select allthat apply)

FRUIT

○ Citrus (Lemon,Lime
   Grapefruit?)

○ Tropical (Pineapple,
   Melon,Lychee)

○ Red (Raspberrry,
   Strawberry,Cherrry)

○ Blue (Blueberry)

○ Black (Blackberry,
   Black Currant)

○ Apple

○ Pear

○ Stone Fruit
   (Peach,Apricot)

NON-FRUIT

○ Earth   ○ Vanilla

○ Mushrooms   ○ Spices

○ Mineral   ○ Floral

○ Stone   ○ Herbs

○ Oak   ○ Buttery

OTHER

_____

_____

_____

_____

_____

TASTE

SWEETNESS

○ Tastes Like Candy

○ Dries Out My Mouth

○ Seem Like There's a Little Sugar

ACIDITY

○ Delightfuly Crisp

○ Like Sucking On a Lemon

○ Not Acidic

MOUTH FEEL / TANNINS
(REDS ONLY)

○ Very Smooth

○ A Little Rough Around the Edges

○ Makes Me Have to Lick My Chops

ALCOHOL

○ Not Noticeable

○ A Little Hot

○ Very Hot!

FINISH

○ Short   ○ Long

○ Medium   ○ Very Long

RATE IT !

☆ ☆ ☆ ☆ ☆

WINE TASTING CARD

NAME OF WINE _____

GRAPE VARIETAL(S) _____

WHERE'S IT FROM _____

YEAR _____ WHITE / RED / ROSE (CIRCLE ONE)

LOOK

RED (SELECT ONE)

○ Purple ○ Ruby

○ Orange ○ Garnet

○ Brown

WHITE (SELECT ONE)

○ Straw ○ Amber/

○ Gold   Brown

○ Yellow

IS IT FIZZY?

○ Yes ○ No

ARE THRE ANY

PARTICLES FLOATING

IN THE GLASS?

○ A Lot

○ A Little Sediment

○ All Clear

SMELL (Select allthat apply)

FRUIT

○ Citrus (Lemon,Lime   ○ Black (Blackberry,

   Grapefruit?)   Black Currant)

○ Tropical (Pineapple,   ○ Apple

   Melon,Lychee)   ○ Pear

○ Red (Raspberrry,   ○ Stone Fruit

   Strawberry,Cherrry)   (Peach,Apricot)

○ Blue (Blueberry)

NON-FRUIT   **OTHER**

○ Earth   ○ Vanilla   _____

○ Mushrooms   ○ Spices   _____

○ Mineral   ○ Floral   _____

○ Stone   ○ Herbs   _____

○ Oak   ○ Buttery   _____

TASTE

SWEETNESS

○ Tastes Like Candy

○ Dries Out My Mouth

○ Seem Like There's a Little Sugar

ACIDITY

○ Delightfuly Crisp

○ Like Sucking On a Lemon

○ Not Acidic

MOUTH FEEL / TANNINS

(REDS ONLY)

○ Very Smooth

○ A Little Rough Around the Edges

○ Makes Me Have to Lick My Chops

ALCOHOL

○ Not Noticeable

○ A Little Hot

○ Very Hot!

FINISH

○ Short   ○ Long

○ Medium   ○ Very Long

RATE IT !

✫ ✫ ✫ ✫ ✫

WINE TASTING CARD

NAME OF WINE _____

GRAPE VARIETAL(S) _____

WHERE'S IT FROM _____

YEAR _____ WHITE / RED / ROSE (CIRCLE ONE)

LOOK

RED (SELECT ONE)

○ Purple   ○ Ruby

○ Orange   ○ Garnet

○ Brown

WHITE (SELECT ONE)

○ Straw   ○ Amber/

○ Gold   Brown

○ Yellow

IS IT FIZZY?

○ Yes   ○ No

ARE THRE ANY

PARTICLES FLOATING

IN THE GLASS?

○ A Lot

○ A Little Sediment

○ All Clear

SMELL   (Select allthat apply)

FRUIT

○ Citrus (Lemon,Lime   ○ Black (Blackberry,

  Grapefruit?)   Black Currant)

○ Tropical (Pineapple,   ○ Apple

  Melon,Lychee)   ○ Pear

○ Red (Raspberrry,   ○ Stone Fruit

  Strawberry,Cherrry)   (Peach,Apricot)

○ Blue (Blueberry)

NON-FRUIT   ### OTHER

○ Earth   ○ Vanilla   _____

○ Mushrooms   ○ Spices   _____

○ Mineral   ○ Floral   _____

○ Stone   ○ Herbs   _____

○ Oak   ○ Buttery   _____

TASTE

SWEETNESS

○ Tastes Like Candy

○ Dries Out My Mouth

○ Seem Like There's a Little Sugar

ACIDITY

○ Delightfuly Crisp

○ Like Sucking On a Lemon

○ Not Acidic

MOUTH FEEL / TANNINS

(REDS ONLY)

○ Very Smooth

○ A Little Rough Around the Edges

○ Makes Me Have to Lick My Chops

ALCOHOL

○ Not Noticeable

○ A Little Hot

○ Very Hot!

FINISH

○ Short   ○ Long

○ Medium   ○ Very Long

RATE IT !

☆ ☆ ☆ ☆ ☆

WINE TASTING CARD

NAME OF WINE _____

GRAPE VARIETAL(S) _____

WHERE'S IT FROM _____

YEAR _____ WHITE / RED / ROSE (CIRCLE ONE)

LOOK

RED (SELECT ONE)

○ Purple   ○ Ruby

○ Orange   ○ Garnet

○ Brown

WHITE (SELECT ONE)

○ Straw   ○ Amber/

○ Gold   Brown

○ Yellow

IS IT FIZZY?

○ Yes   ○ No

ARE THRE ANY

PARTICLES FLOATING

IN THE GLASS?

○ A Lot

○ A Little Sediment

○ All Clear

SMELL   (Select allthat apply)

FRUIT

○ Citrus (Lemon,Lime Grapefruit?)

○ Tropical (Pineapple, Melon,Lychee)

○ Red (Raspberrry, Strawberry,Cherrry)

○ Blue (Blueberry)

○ Black (Blackberry, Black Currant)

○ Apple

○ Pear

○ Stone Fruit (Peach,Apricot)

NON-FRUIT

○ Earth   ○ Vanilla

○ Mushrooms   ○ Spices

○ Mineral   ○ Floral

○ Stone   ○ Herbs

○ Oak   ○ Buttery

OTHER

_____

_____

_____

_____

_____

TASTE

SWEETNESS

○ Tastes Like Candy

○ Dries Out My Mouth

○ Seem Like There's a Little Sugar

ACIDITY

○ Delightfuly Crisp

○ Like Sucking On a Lemon

○ Not Acidic

MOUTH FEEL / TANNINS

(REDS ONLY)

○ Very Smooth

○ A Little Rough Around the Edges

○ Makes Me Have to Lick My Chops

ALCOHOL

○ Not Noticeable

○ A Little Hot

○ Very Hot!

FINISH

○ Short   ○ Long

○ Medium   ○ Very Long

RATE IT !

☆ ☆ ☆ ☆ ☆

WINE TASTING CARD

NAME OF WINE _____

GRAPE VARIETAL(S) _____

WHERE'S IT FROM _____

YEAR _____ WHITE / RED / ROSE (CIRCLE ONE)

LOOK

RED (SELECT ONE)
- ○ Purple   ○ Ruby
- ○ Orange   ○ Garnet
- ○ Brown

WHITE (SELECT ONE)
- ○ Straw   ○ Amber/
- ○ Gold   Brown
- ○ Yellow

IS IT FIZZY?
- ○ Yes   ○ No

ARE THRE ANY PARTICLES FLOATING IN THE GLASS?
- ○ A Lot
- ○ A Little Sediment
- ○ All Clear

SMELL   (Select allthat apply)

FRUIT
- ○ Citrus (Lemon,Lime Grapefruit?)
- ○ Tropical (Pineapple, Melon,Lychee)
- ○ Red (Raspberrry, Strawberry,Cherrry)
- ○ Blue (Blueberry)
- ○ Black (Blackberry, Black Currant)
- ○ Apple
- ○ Pear
- ○ Stone Fruit (Peach,Apricot)

NON-FRUIT
- ○ Earth
- ○ Mushrooms
- ○ Mineral
- ○ Stone
- ○ Oak
- ○ Vanilla
- ○ Spices
- ○ Floral
- ○ Herbs
- ○ Buttery

OTHER
_____
_____
_____
_____
_____

TASTE

SWEETNESS
- ○ Tastes Like Candy
- ○ Dries Out My Mouth
- ○ Seem Like There's a Little Sugar

ACIDITY
- ○ Delightfuly Crisp
- ○ Like Sucking On a Lemon
- ○ Not Acidic

MOUTH FEEL / TANNINS (REDS ONLY)
- ○ Very Smooth
- ○ A Little Rough Around the Edges
- ○ Makes Me Have to Lick My Chops

ALCOHOL
- ○ Not Noticeable
- ○ A Little Hot
- ○ Very Hot!

FINISH
- ○ Short   ○ Long
- ○ Medium   ○ Very Long

RATE IT !

★ ★ ★ ★ ★

WINE TASTING CARD

NAME OF WINE _____

GRAPE VARIETAL(S) _____

WHERE'S IT FROM _____

YEAR _____ WHITE / RED / ROSE (CIRCLE ONE)

LOOK

RED (SELECT ONE)

○ Purple ○ Ruby

○ Orange ○ Garnet

○ Brown

WHITE (SELECT ONE)

○ Straw ○ Amber/

○ Gold   Brown

○ Yellow

IS IT FIZZY?

○ Yes ○ No

ARE THRE ANY

PARTICLES FLOATING

IN THE GLASS?

○ A Lot

○ A Little Sediment

○ All Clear

SMELL (Select allthat apply)

FRUIT

○ Citrus (Lemon,Lime

     Grapefruit?)

○ Tropical (Pineapple,

     Melon,Lychee)

○ Red (Raspberrry,

     Strawberry,Cherrry)

○ Blue (Blueberry)

○ Black (Blackberry,

     Black Currant)

○ Apple

○ Pear

○ Stone Fruit

     (Peach,Apricot)

NON-FRUIT

○ Earth ○ Vanilla

○ Mushrooms ○ Spices

○ Mineral ○ Floral

○ Stone ○ Herbs

○ Oak ○ Buttery

OTHER

_____

_____

_____

_____

_____

TASTE

SWEETNESS

○ Tastes Like Candy

○ Dries Out My Mouth

○ Seem Like There's a Little Sugar

ACIDITY

○ Delightfuly Crisp

○ Like Sucking On a Lemon

○ Not Acidic

MOUTH FEEL / TANNINS

(REDS ONLY)

○ Very Smooth

○ A Little Rough Around the Edges

○ Makes Me Have to Lick My Chops

ALCOHOL

○ Not Noticeable

○ A Little Hot

○ Very Hot!

FINISH

○ Short ○ Long

○ Medium ○ Very Long

RATE IT !

☆ ☆ ☆ ☆ ☆

WINE TASTING CARD

NAME OF WINE _____

GRAPE VARIETAL(S) _____

WHERE'S IT FROM _____

YEAR _____ WHITE / RED / ROSE (CIRCLE ONE)

LOOK

RED (SELECT ONE)

- ○ Purple
- ○ Ruby
- ○ Orange
- ○ Garnet
- ○ Brown

WHITE (SELECT ONE)

- ○ Straw
- ○ Amber/
- ○ Gold   Brown
- ○ Yellow

IS IT FIZZY?

- ○ Yes   ○ No

ARE THRE ANY
PARTICLES FLOATING
IN THE GLASS?

- ○ A Lot
- ○ A Little Sediment
- ○ All Clear

SMELL   (Select allthat apply)

FRUIT

- ○ Citrus (Lemon,Lime Grapefruit?)
- ○ Tropical (Pineapple, Melon,Lychee)
- ○ Red (Raspberrry, Strawberry,Cherrry)
- ○ Blue (Blueberry)
- ○ Black (Blackberry, Black Currant)
- ○ Apple
- ○ Pear
- ○ Stone Fruit (Peach,Apricot)

NON-FRUIT

- ○ Earth
- ○ Mushrooms
- ○ Mineral
- ○ Stone
- ○ Oak
- ○ Vanilla
- ○ Spices
- ○ Floral
- ○ Herbs
- ○ Buttery

OTHER

- _____
- _____
- _____
- _____

TASTE

SWEETNESS

- ○ Tastes Like Candy
- ○ Dries Out My Mouth
- ○ Seem Like There's a Little Sugar

ACIDITY

- ○ Delightfuly Crisp
- ○ Like Sucking On a Lemon
- ○ Not Acidic

MOUTH FEEL / TANNINS
(REDS ONLY)

- ○ Very Smooth
- ○ A Little Rough Around the Edges
- ○ Makes Me Have to Lick My Chops

ALCOHOL

- ○ Not Noticeable
- ○ A Little Hot
- ○ Very Hot!

FINISH

- ○ Short   ○ Long
- ○ Medium   ○ Very Long

RATE IT !

★ ★ ★ ★ ★

WINE TASTING CARD

NAME OF WINE _____

GRAPE VARIETAL(S) _____

WHERE'S IT FROM _____

YEAR _____ WHITE / RED / ROSE (CIRCLE ONE)

LOOK

RED (SELECT ONE)

- ○ Purple   ○ Ruby
- ○ Orange   ○ Garnet
- ○ Brown

WHITE (SELECT ONE)

- ○ Straw   ○ Amber/
- ○ Gold   Brown
- ○ Yellow

IS IT FIZZY?

- ○ Yes   ○ No

ARE THRE ANY PARTICLES FLOATING IN THE GLASS?

- ○ A Lot
- ○ A Little Sediment
- ○ All Clear

SMELL   (Select allthat apply)

FRUIT

- ○ Citrus (Lemon,Lime Grapefruit?)
- ○ Tropical (Pineapple, Melon,Lychee)
- ○ Red (Raspberrry, Strawberry,Cherrry)
- ○ Blue (Blueberry)

- ○ Black (Blackberry, Black Currant)
- ○ Apple
- ○ Pear
- ○ Stone Fruit (Peach,Apricot)

NON-FRUIT

- ○ Earth
- ○ Mushrooms
- ○ Mineral
- ○ Stone
- ○ Oak

- ○ Vanilla
- ○ Spices
- ○ Floral
- ○ Herbs
- ○ Buttery

OTHER

_____
_____
_____
_____
_____

TASTE

SWEETNESS

- ○ Tastes Like Candy
- ○ Dries Out My Mouth
- ○ Seem Like There's a Little Sugar

ACIDITY

- ○ Delightfuly Crisp
- ○ Like Sucking On a Lemon
- ○ Not Acidic

MOUTH FEEL / TANNINS (REDS ONLY)

- ○ Very Smooth
- ○ A Little Rough Around the Edges
- ○ Makes Me Have to Lick My Chops

ALCOHOL

- ○ Not Noticeable
- ○ A Little Hot
- ○ Very Hot!

FINISH

- ○ Short   ○ Long
- ○ Medium   ○ Very Long

RATE IT !

☆ ☆ ☆ ☆ ☆

WINE TASTING CARD

NAME OF WINE _____

GRAPE VARIETAL(S) _____

WHERE'S IT FROM _____

YEAR _____ WHITE / RED / ROSE (CIRCLE ONE)

LOOK

RED (SELECT ONE)
- ○ Purple ○ Ruby
- ○ Orange ○ Garnet
- ○ Brown

WHITE (SELECT ONE)
- ○ Straw ○ Amber/
- ○ Gold   Brown
- ○ Yellow

IS IT FIZZY?
- ○ Yes   ○ No

ARE THRE ANY PARTICLES FLOATING IN THE GLASS?
- ○ A Lot
- ○ A Little Sediment
- ○ All Clear

SMELL (Select allthat apply)

FRUIT
- ○ Citrus (Lemon,Lime Grapefruit?)
- ○ Tropical (Pineapple, Melon,Lychee)
- ○ Red (Raspberrry, Strawberry,Cherrry)
- ○ Blue (Blueberry)

- ○ Black (Blackberry, Black Currant)
- ○ Apple
- ○ Pear
- ○ Stone Fruit (Peach,Apricot)

NON-FRUIT
- ○ Earth
- ○ Mushrooms
- ○ Mineral
- ○ Stone
- ○ Oak

- ○ Vanilla
- ○ Spices
- ○ Floral
- ○ Herbs
- ○ Buttery

OTHER
- _____
- _____
- _____
- _____
- _____

TASTE

SWEETNESS
- ○ Tastes Like Candy
- ○ Dries Out My Mouth
- ○ Seem Like There's a Little Sugar

ACIDITY
- ○ Delightfuly Crisp
- ○ Like Sucking On a Lemon
- ○ Not Acidic

MOUTH FEEL / TANNINS (REDS ONLY)
- ○ Very Smooth
- ○ A Little Rough Around the Edges
- ○ Makes Me Have to Lick My Chops

ALCOHOL
- ○ Not Noticeable
- ○ A Little Hot
- ○ Very Hot!

FINISH
- ○ Short   ○ Long
- ○ Medium ○ Very Long

RATE IT !

☆ ☆ ☆ ☆ ☆

WINE TASTING CARD

NAME OF WINE _____

GRAPE VARIETAL(S) _____

WHERE'S IT FROM _____

YEAR _____   WHITE / RED / ROSE (CIRCLE ONE)

LOOK

RED (SELECT ONE)
- ○ Purple   ○ Ruby
- ○ Orange   ○ Garnet
- ○ Brown

WHITE (SELECT ONE)
- ○ Straw   ○ Amber/
- ○ Gold   Brown
- ○ Yellow

IS IT FIZZY?
- ○ Yes   ○ No

ARE THRE ANY
PARTICLES FLOATING
IN THE GLASS?
- ○ A Lot
- ○ A Little Sediment
- ○ All Clear

SMELL   (Select allthat apply)

FRUIT
- ○ Citrus (Lemon,Lime Grapefruit?)
- ○ Tropical (Pineapple, Melon,Lychee)
- ○ Red (Raspberrry, Strawberry,Cherrry)
- ○ Blue (Blueberry)

- ○ Black (Blackberry, Black Currant)
- ○ Apple
- ○ Pear
- ○ Stone Fruit (Peach,Apricot)

NON-FRUIT
- ○ Earth
- ○ Mushrooms
- ○ Mineral
- ○ Stone
- ○ Oak

- ○ Vanilla
- ○ Spices
- ○ Floral
- ○ Herbs
- ○ Buttery

OTHER
_____
_____
_____
_____
_____

TASTE

SWEETNESS
- ○ Tastes Like Candy
- ○ Dries Out My Mouth
- ○ Seem Like There's a Little Sugar

ACIDITY
- ○ Delightfuly Crisp
- ○ Like Sucking On a Lemon
- ○ Not Acidic

MOUTH FEEL / TANNINS (REDS ONLY)
- ○ Very Smooth
- ○ A Little Rough Around the Edges
- ○ Makes Me Have to Lick My Chops

ALCOHOL
- ○ Not Noticeable
- ○ A Little Hot
- ○ Very Hot!

FINISH
- ○ Short   ○ Long
- ○ Medium   ○ Very Long

RATE IT !

★ ★ ★ ★ ★

WINE TASTING CARD

NAME OF WINE _____

GRAPE VARIETAL(S) _____

WHERE'S IT FROM _____

YEAR _____   WHITE / RED / ROSE (CIRCLE ONE)

LOOK

RED (SELECT ONE)

○ Purple   ○ Ruby

○ Orange   ○ Garnet

○ Brown

WHITE (SELECT ONE)

○ Straw   ○ Amber/

○ Gold   Brown

○ Yellow

IS IT FIZZY?

○ Yes   ○ No

ARE THRE ANY

PARTICLES FLOATING

IN THE GLASS?

○ A Lot

○ A Little Sediment

○ All Clear

SMELL   (Select allthat apply)

FRUIT

○ Citrus (Lemon,Lime   ○ Black (Blackberry,

Grapefruit?)   Black Currant)

○ Tropical (Pineapple,   ○ Apple

Melon,Lychee)   ○ Pear

○ Red (Raspberrry,   ○ Stone Fruit

Strawberry,Cherrry)   (Peach,Apricot)

○ Blue (Blueberry)

NON-FRUIT   **OTHER**

○ Earth   ○ Vanilla   _____

○ Mushrooms ○ Spices   _____

○ Mineral   ○ Floral   _____

○ Stone   ○ Herbs   _____

○ Oak   ○ Buttery   _____

TASTE

SWEETNESS

○ Tastes Like Candy

○ Dries Out My Mouth

○ Seem Like There's a Little Sugar

ACIDITY

○ Delightfuly Crisp

○ Like Sucking On a Lemon

○ Not Acidic

MOUTH FEEL / TANNINS

(REDS ONLY)

○ Very Smooth

○ A Little Rough Around the Edges

○ Makes Me Have to Lick My Chops

ALCOHOL

○ Not Noticeable

○ A Little Hot

○ Very Hot!

FINISH

○ Short   ○ Long

○ Medium   ○ Very Long

RATE IT !

★ ★ ★ ★ ★

WINE TASTING CARD

NAME OF WINE _____

GRAPE VARIETAL(S) _____

WHERE'S IT FROM _____

YEAR _____ WHITE / RED / ROSE (CIRCLE ONE)

LOOK

RED (SELECT ONE)

○ Purple   ○ Ruby

○ Orange   ○ Garnet

○ Brown

WHITE (SELECT ONE)

○ Straw   ○ Amber/

○ Gold   Brown

○ Yellow

IS IT FIZZY?

○ Yes   ○ No

ARE THRE ANY

PARTICLES FLOATING

IN THE GLASS?

○ A Lot

○ A Little Sediment

○ All Clear

SMELL   (Select allthat apply)

FRUIT

○ Citrus (Lemon,Lime   ○ Black (Blackberry,

   Grapefruit?)   Black Currant)

○ Tropical (Pineapple,   ○ Apple

   Melon,Lychee)   ○ Pear

○ Red (Raspberrry,   ○ Stone Fruit

   Strawberry,Cherrry)   (Peach,Apricot)

○ Blue (Blueberry)

NON-FRUIT   OTHER

○ Earth   ○ Vanilla   _____

○ Mushrooms ○ Spices   _____

○ Mineral   ○ Floral   _____

○ Stone   ○ Herbs   _____

○ Oak   ○ Buttery   _____

TASTE

SWEETNESS

○ Tastes Like Candy

○ Dries Out My Mouth

○ Seem Like There's a Little Sugar

ACIDITY

○ Delightfuly Crisp

○ Like Sucking On a Lemon

○ Not Acidic

MOUTH FEEL / TANNINS

(REDS ONLY)

○ Very Smooth

○ A Little Rough Around the Edges

○ Makes Me Have to Lick My Chops

ALCOHOL

○ Not Noticeable

○ A Little Hot

○ Very Hot!

FINISH

○ Short   ○ Long

○ Medium   ○ Very Long

RATE IT !

☆ ☆ ☆ ☆ ☆

WINE TASTING CARD

NAME OF WINE _____

GRAPE VARIETAL(S) _____

WHERE'S IT FROM _____

YEAR _____ WHITE / RED / ROSE (CIRCLE ONE)

LOOK

RED (SELECT ONE)

- ○ Purple   ○ Ruby
- ○ Orange   ○ Garnet
- ○ Brown

WHITE (SELECT ONE)

- ○ Straw   ○ Amber/
- ○ Gold   Brown
- ○ Yellow

IS IT FIZZY?

- ○ Yes   ○ No

ARE THRE ANY

PARTICLES FLOATING

IN THE GLASS?

- ○ A Lot
- ○ A Little Sediment
- ○ All Clear

SMELL   (Select allthat apply)

FRUIT

- ○ Citrus (Lemon,Lime Grapefruit?)
- ○ Tropical (Pineapple, Melon,Lychee)
- ○ Red (Raspberrry, Strawberry,Cherrry)
- ○ Blue (Blueberry)

- ○ Black (Blackberry, Black Currant)
- ○ Apple
- ○ Pear
- ○ Stone Fruit (Peach,Apricot)

NON-FRUIT

- ○ Earth
- ○ Mushrooms
- ○ Mineral
- ○ Stone
- ○ Oak

- ○ Vanilla
- ○ Spices
- ○ Floral
- ○ Herbs
- ○ Buttery

OTHER

_____

_____

_____

_____

_____

TASTE

SWEETNESS

- ○ Tastes Like Candy
- ○ Dries Out My Mouth
- ○ Seem Like There's a Little Sugar

ACIDITY

- ○ Delightfuly Crisp
- ○ Like Sucking On a Lemon
- ○ Not Acidic

MOUTH FEEL / TANNINS

(REDS ONLY)

- ○ Very Smooth
- ○ A Little Rough Around the Edges
- ○ Makes Me Have to Lick My Chops

ALCOHOL

- ○ Not Noticeable
- ○ A Little Hot
- ○ Very Hot!

FINISH

- ○ Short   ○ Long
- ○ Medium   ○ Very Long

RATE IT !

☆ ☆ ☆ ☆ ☆

WINE TASTING CARD

NAME OF WINE _____

GRAPE VARIETAL(S) _____

WHERE'S IT FROM _____

YEAR _____ WHITE / RED / ROSE (CIRCLE ONE)

LOOK

TASTE

RED (SELECT ONE)

- ○ Purple   ○ Ruby
- ○ Orange   ○ Garnet
- ○ Brown

IS IT FIZZY?

- ○ Yes   ○ No

ARE THRE ANY

PARTICLES FLOATING

IN THE GLASS?

WHITE (SELECT ONE)

- ○ Straw   ○ Amber/
- ○ Gold   Brown
- ○ Yellow

- ○ A Lot
- ○ A Little Sediment
- ○ All Clear

SWEETNESS

- ○ Tastes Like Candy
- ○ Dries Out My Mouth
- ○ Seem Like There's a Little Sugar

ACIDITY

- ○ Delightfuly Crisp
- ○ Like Sucking On a Lemon
- ○ Not Acidic

MOUTH FEEL / TANNINS

(REDS ONLY)

- ○ Very Smooth
- ○ A Little Rough Around the Edges
- ○ Makes Me Have to Lick My Chops

SMELL   (Select allthat apply)

FRUIT

- ○ Citrus (Lemon,Lime Grapefruit?)
- ○ Tropical (Pineapple, Melon,Lychee)
- ○ Red (Raspberrry, Strawberry,Cherrry)
- ○ Blue (Blueberry)

- ○ Black (Blackberry, Black Currant)
- ○ Apple
- ○ Pear
- ○ Stone Fruit (Peach,Apricot)

ALCOHOL

- ○ Not Noticeable
- ○ A Little Hot
- ○ Very Hot!

FINISH

- ○ Short   ○ Long
- ○ Medium   ○ Very Long

NON-FRUIT

- ○ Earth
- ○ Mushrooms
- ○ Mineral
- ○ Stone
- ○ Oak

- ○ Vanilla
- ○ Spices
- ○ Floral
- ○ Herbs
- ○ Buttery

OTHER

_____

_____

_____

_____

RATE IT !

☆ ☆ ☆ ☆ ☆

WINE TASTING CARD

NAME OF WINE _____

GRAPE VARIETAL(S) _____

WHERE'S IT FROM _____

YEAR _____ WHITE / RED / ROSE (CIRCLE ONE)

LOOK

RED (SELECT ONE)

○ Purple   ○ Ruby

○ Orange   ○ Garnet

○ Brown

WHITE (SELECT ONE)

○ Straw   ○ Amber/

○ Gold   Brown

○ Yellow

IS IT FIZZY?

○ Yes   ○ No

ARE THRE ANY

PARTICLES FLOATING

IN THE GLASS?

○ A Lot

○ A Little Sediment

○ All Clear

SMELL   (Select allthat apply)

FRUIT

○ Citrus (Lemon,Lime   ○ Black (Blackberry,

   Grapefruit?)   Black Currant)

○ Tropical (Pineapple,   ○ Apple

   Melon,Lychee)   ○ Pear

○ Red (Raspberrry,   ○ Stone Fruit

   Strawberry,Cherrry)   (Peach,Apricot)

○ Blue (Blueberry)

NON-FRUIT   **OTHER**

○ Earth   ○ Vanilla   _____

○ Mushrooms ○ Spices   _____

○ Mineral   ○ Floral   _____

○ Stone   ○ Herbs   _____

○ Oak   ○ Buttery   _____

TASTE

SWEETNESS

○ Tastes Like Candy

○ Dries Out My Mouth

○ Seem Like There's a Little Sugar

ACIDITY

○ Delightfuly Crisp

○ Like Sucking On a Lemon

○ Not Acidic

MOUTH FEEL / TANNINS

(REDS ONLY)

○ Very Smooth

○ A Little Rough Around the Edges

○ Makes Me Have to Lick My Chops

ALCOHOL

○ Not Noticeable

○ A Little Hot

○ Very Hot!

FINISH

○ Short   ○ Long

○ Medium   ○ Very Long

RATE IT !

☆ ☆ ☆ ☆ ☆

WINE TASTING CARD

NAME OF WINE _____

GRAPE VARIETAL(S) _____

WHERE'S IT FROM _____

YEAR _____ WHITE / RED / ROSE (CIRCLE ONE)

LOOK

RED (SELECT ONE)

- ○ Purple   ○ Ruby
- ○ Orange   ○ Garnet
- ○ Brown

WHITE (SELECT ONE)

- ○ Straw   ○ Amber/
- ○ Gold   Brown
- ○ Yellow

IS IT FIZZY?

- ○ Yes   ○ No

ARE THRE ANY

PARTICLES FLOATING

IN THE GLASS?

- ○ A Lot
- ○ A Little Sediment
- ○ All Clear

SMELL   (Select allthat apply)

FRUIT

- ○ Citrus (Lemon,Lime Grapefruit?)
- ○ Tropical (Pineapple, Melon,Lychee)
- ○ Red (Raspberrry, Strawberry,Cherrry)
- ○ Blue (Blueberry)

- ○ Black (Blackberry, Black Currant)
- ○ Apple
- ○ Pear
- ○ Stone Fruit (Peach,Apricot)

NON-FRUIT

- ○ Earth
- ○ Mushrooms
- ○ Mineral
- ○ Stone
- ○ Oak

- ○ Vanilla
- ○ Spices
- ○ Floral
- ○ Herbs
- ○ Buttery

OTHER

_____
_____
_____
_____
_____

TASTE

SWEETNESS

- ○ Tastes Like Candy
- ○ Dries Out My Mouth
- ○ Seem Like There's a Little Sugar

ACIDITY

- ○ Delightfuly Crisp
- ○ Like Sucking On a Lemon
- ○ Not Acidic

MOUTH FEEL / TANNINS

(REDS ONLY)

- ○ Very Smooth
- ○ A Little Rough Around the Edges
- ○ Makes Me Have to Lick My Chops

ALCOHOL

- ○ Not Noticeable
- ○ A Little Hot
- ○ Very Hot!

FINISH

- ○ Short   ○ Long
- ○ Medium   ○ Very Long

RATE IT !

☆ ☆ ☆ ☆ ☆

WINE TASTING CARD

NAME OF WINE _____

GRAPE VARIETAL(S) _____

WHERE'S IT FROM _____

YEAR _____ WHITE / RED / ROSE (CIRCLE ONE)

LOOK

RED (SELECT ONE)

- ○ Purple   ○ Ruby
- ○ Orange   ○ Garnet
- ○ Brown

WHITE (SELECT ONE)

- ○ Straw   ○ Amber/
- ○ Gold   Brown
- ○ Yellow

IS IT FIZZY?

- ○ Yes   ○ No

ARE THRE ANY PARTICLES FLOATING IN THE GLASS?

- ○ A Lot
- ○ A Little Sediment
- ○ All Clear

SMELL (Select allthat apply)

FRUIT

- ○ Citrus (Lemon,Lime Grapefruit?)
- ○ Tropical (Pineapple, Melon,Lychee)
- ○ Red (Raspberrry, Strawberry,Cherrry)
- ○ Blue (Blueberry)
- ○ Black (Blackberry, Black Currant)
- ○ Apple
- ○ Pear
- ○ Stone Fruit (Peach,Apricot)

NON-FRUIT

- ○ Earth   ○ Vanilla
- ○ Mushrooms   ○ Spices
- ○ Mineral   ○ Floral
- ○ Stone   ○ Herbs
- ○ Oak   ○ Buttery

OTHER

_____

_____

_____

_____

_____

TASTE

SWEETNESS

- ○ Tastes Like Candy
- ○ Dries Out My Mouth
- ○ Seem Like There's a Little Sugar

ACIDITY

- ○ Delightfuly Crisp
- ○ Like Sucking On a Lemon
- ○ Not Acidic

MOUTH FEEL / TANNINS (REDS ONLY)

- ○ Very Smooth
- ○ A Little Rough Around the Edges
- ○ Makes Me Have to Lick My Chops

ALCOHOL

- ○ Not Noticeable
- ○ A Little Hot
- ○ Very Hot!

FINISH

- ○ Short   ○ Long
- ○ Medium   ○ Very Long

RATE IT !

☆ ☆ ☆ ☆ ☆

WINE TASTING CARD

NAME OF WINE   _____

GRAPE VARIETAL(S)   _____

WHERE'S IT FROM   _____

YEAR   _____   WHITE / RED / ROSE (CIRCLE ONE)

LOOK

TASTE

RED (SELECT ONE)

- ○ Purple   ○ Ruby
- ○ Orange   ○ Garnet
- ○ Brown

WHITE (SELECT ONE)

- ○ Straw   ○ Amber/
- ○ Gold   Brown
- ○ Yellow

IS IT FIZZY?

- ○ Yes   ○ No

ARE THRE ANY

PARTICLES FLOATING

IN THE GLASS?

- ○ A Lot
- ○ A Little Sediment
- ○ All Clear

SWEETNESS

- ○ Tastes Like Candy
- ○ Dries Out My Mouth
- ○ Seem Like There's a Little Sugar

ACIDITY

- ○ Delightfuly Crisp
- ○ Like Sucking On a Lemon
- ○ Not Acidic

MOUTH FEEL / TANNINS

(REDS ONLY)

- ○ Very Smooth
- ○ A Little Rough Around the Edges
- ○ Makes Me Have to Lick My Chops

ALCOHOL

- ○ Not Noticeable
- ○ A Little Hot
- ○ Very Hot!

SMELL (Select allthat apply)

FRUIT

- ○ Citrus (Lemon,Lime Grapefruit?)
- ○ Tropical (Pineapple, Melon,Lychee)
- ○ Red (Raspberrry, Strawberry,Cherrry)
- ○ Blue (Blueberry)

- ○ Black (Blackberry, Black Currant)
- ○ Apple
- ○ Pear
- ○ Stone Fruit (Peach,Apricot)

FINISH

- ○ Short   ○ Long
- ○ Medium   ○ Very Long

NON-FRUIT

- ○ Earth   ○ Vanilla
- ○ Mushrooms   ○ Spices
- ○ Mineral   ○ Floral
- ○ Stone   ○ Herbs
- ○ Oak   ○ Buttery

OTHER

_____

_____

_____

_____

_____

RATE IT !

☆ ☆ ☆ ☆ ☆

WINE TASTING CARD

NAME OF WINE _____

GRAPE VARIETAL(S) _____

WHERE'S IT FROM _____

YEAR _____ WHITE / RED / ROSE (CIRCLE ONE)

LOOK

RED (SELECT ONE)

○ Purple   ○ Ruby

○ Orange   ○ Garnet

○ Brown

WHITE (SELECT ONE)

○ Straw   ○ Amber/

○ Gold   Brown

○ Yellow

IS IT FIZZY?

○ Yes   ○ No

ARE THRE ANY

PARTICLES FLOATING

IN THE GLASS?

○ A Lot

○ A Little Sediment

○ All Clear

SMELL   (Select allthat apply)

FRUIT

○ Citrus (Lemon,Lime   ○ Black (Blackberry,

  Grapefruit?)   Black Currant)

○ Tropical (Pineapple,   ○ Apple

  Melon,Lychee)   ○ Pear

○ Red (Raspberrry,   ○ Stone Fruit

  Strawberry,Cherrry)   (Peach,Apricot)

○ Blue (Blueberry)

NON-FRUIT   **OTHER**

○ Earth   ○ Vanilla   _____

○ Mushrooms ○ Spices   _____

○ Mineral   ○ Floral   _____

○ Stone   ○ Herbs   _____

○ Oak   ○ Buttery   _____

TASTE

SWEETNESS

○ Tastes Like Candy

○ Dries Out My Mouth

○ Seem Like There's a Little Sugar

ACIDITY

○ Delightfuly Crisp

○ Like Sucking On a Lemon

○ Not Acidic

MOUTH FEEL / TANNINS

(REDS ONLY)

○ Very Smooth

○ A Little Rough Around the Edges

○ Makes Me Have to Lick My Chops

ALCOHOL

○ Not Noticeable

○ A Little Hot

○ Very Hot!

FINISH

○ Short   ○ Long

○ Medium   ○ Very Long

RATE IT !

★ ★ ★ ★ ★

WINE TASTING CARD

NAME OF WINE _____

GRAPE VARIETAL(S) _____

WHERE'S IT FROM _____

YEAR _____ WHITE / RED / ROSE (CIRCLE ONE)

LOOK

RED (SELECT ONE)

○ Purple   ○ Ruby

○ Orange   ○ Garnet

○ Brown

WHITE (SELECT ONE)

○ Straw   ○ Amber/

○ Gold   Brown

○ Yellow

IS IT FIZZY?

○ Yes   ○ No

ARE THRE ANY PARTICLES FLOATING IN THE GLASS?

○ A Lot

○ A Little Sediment

○ All Clear

SMELL   (Select allthat apply)

FRUIT

○ Citrus (Lemon,Lime Grapefruit?)

○ Tropical (Pineapple, Melon,Lychee)

○ Red (Raspberrry, Strawberry,Cherrry)

○ Blue (Blueberry)

○ Black (Blackberry, Black Currant)

○ Apple

○ Pear

○ Stone Fruit (Peach,Apricot)

NON-FRUIT

○ Earth

○ Mushrooms

○ Mineral

○ Stone

○ Oak

○ Vanilla

○ Spices

○ Floral

○ Herbs

○ Buttery

OTHER

_____

_____

_____

_____

TASTE

SWEETNESS

○ Tastes Like Candy

○ Dries Out My Mouth

○ Seem Like There's a Little Sugar

ACIDITY

○ Delightfuly Crisp

○ Like Sucking On a Lemon

○ Not Acidic

MOUTH FEEL / TANNINS (REDS ONLY)

○ Very Smooth

○ A Little Rough Around the Edges

○ Makes Me Have to Lick My Chops

ALCOHOL

○ Not Noticeable

○ A Little Hot

○ Very Hot!

FINISH

○ Short   ○ Long

○ Medium   ○ Very Long

RATE IT !

☆ ☆ ☆ ☆ ☆

WINE TASTING CARD

NAME OF WINE _____

GRAPE VARIETAL(S) _____

WHERE'S IT FROM _____

YEAR _____ WHITE / RED / ROSE (CIRCLE ONE)

LOOK

RED (SELECT ONE)

○ Purple   ○ Ruby

○ Orange   ○ Garnet

○ Brown

WHITE (SELECT ONE)

○ Straw   ○ Amber/

○ Gold   Brown

○ Yellow

IS IT FIZZY?

○ Yes   ○ No

ARE THRE ANY
PARTICLES FLOATING
IN THE GLASS?

○ A Lot

○ A Little Sediment

○ All Clear

SMELL   (Select allthat apply)

FRUIT

○ Citrus (Lemon,Lime
   Grapefruit?)

○ Tropical (Pineapple,
   Melon,Lychee)

○ Red (Raspberrry,
   Strawberry,Cherrry)

○ Blue (Blueberry)

○ Black (Blackberry,
   Black Currant)

○ Apple

○ Pear

○ Stone Fruit
   (Peach,Apricot)

NON-FRUIT

○ Earth

○ Mushrooms

○ Mineral

○ Stone

○ Oak

○ Vanilla

○ Spices

○ Floral

○ Herbs

○ Buttery

OTHER

_____

_____

_____

_____

TASTE

SWEETNESS

○ Tastes Like Candy

○ Dries Out My Mouth

○ Seem Like There's a Little Sugar

ACIDITY

○ Delightfuly Crisp

○ Like Sucking On a Lemon

○ Not Acidic

MOUTH FEEL / TANNINS
(REDS ONLY)

○ Very Smooth

○ A Little Rough Around the Edges

○ Makes Me Have to Lick My Chops

ALCOHOL

○ Not Noticeable

○ A Little Hot

○ Very Hot!

FINISH

○ Short   ○ Long

○ Medium   ○ Very Long

RATE IT !

☆ ☆ ☆ ☆ ☆

WINE TASTING CARD

NAME OF WINE _____

GRAPE VARIETAL(S) _____

WHERE'S IT FROM _____

YEAR _____   WHITE / RED / ROSE (CIRCLE ONE)

LOOK

RED (SELECT ONE)
- ○ Purple   ○ Ruby
- ○ Orange   ○ Garnet
- ○ Brown

WHITE (SELECT ONE)
- ○ Straw   ○ Amber/
- ○ Gold   Brown
- ○ Yellow

IS IT FIZZY?
- ○ Yes   ○ No

ARE THRE ANY PARTICLES FLOATING IN THE GLASS?
- ○ A Lot
- ○ A Little Sediment
- ○ All Clear

SMELL   (Select allthat apply)

FRUIT
- ○ Citrus (Lemon,Lime Grapefruit?)
- ○ Tropical (Pineapple, Melon,Lychee)
- ○ Red (Raspberrry, Strawberry,Cherrry)
- ○ Blue (Blueberry)

- ○ Black (Blackberry, Black Currant)
- ○ Apple
- ○ Pear
- ○ Stone Fruit (Peach,Apricot)

NON-FRUIT
- ○ Earth
- ○ Mushrooms
- ○ Mineral
- ○ Stone
- ○ Oak

- ○ Vanilla
- ○ Spices
- ○ Floral
- ○ Herbs
- ○ Buttery

OTHER
- _____
- _____
- _____
- _____

TASTE

SWEETNESS
- ○ Tastes Like Candy
- ○ Dries Out My Mouth
- ○ Seem Like There's a Little Sugar

ACIDITY
- ○ Delightfuly Crisp
- ○ Like Sucking On a Lemon
- ○ Not Acidic

MOUTH FEEL / TANNINS (REDS ONLY)
- ○ Very Smooth
- ○ A Little Rough Around the Edges
- ○ Makes Me Have to Lick My Chops

ALCOHOL
- ○ Not Noticeable
- ○ A Little Hot
- ○ Very Hot!

FINISH
- ○ Short   ○ Long
- ○ Medium   ○ Very Long

RATE IT !

☆ ☆ ☆ ☆ ☆

WINE TASTING CARD

NAME OF WINE _____

GRAPE VARIETAL(S) _____

WHERE'S IT FROM _____

YEAR _____ WHITE / RED / ROSE (CIRCLE ONE)

LOOK

RED (SELECT ONE)

○ Purple   ○ Ruby

○ Orange   ○ Garnet

○ Brown

WHITE (SELECT ONE)

○ Straw   ○ Amber/

○ Gold   Brown

○ Yellow

IS IT FIZZY?

○ Yes   ○ No

ARE THRE ANY

PARTICLES FLOATING

IN THE GLASS?

○ A Lot

○ A Little Sediment

○ All Clear

SMELL   (Select allthat apply)

FRUIT

○ Citrus (Lemon,Lime

  Grapefruit?)

○ Tropical (Pineapple,

  Melon,Lychee)

○ Red (Raspberrry,

  Strawberry,Cherrry)

○ Blue (Blueberry)

○ Black (Blackberry,

  Black Currant)

○ Apple

○ Pear

○ Stone Fruit

  (Peach,Apricot)

NON-FRUIT

○ Earth

○ Mushrooms

○ Mineral

○ Stone

○ Oak

○ Vanilla

○ Spices

○ Floral

○ Herbs

○ Buttery

OTHER

_____

_____

_____

_____

_____

TASTE

SWEETNESS

○ Tastes Like Candy

○ Dries Out My Mouth

○ Seem Like There's a Little Sugar

ACIDITY

○ Delightfuly Crisp

○ Like Sucking On a Lemon

○ Not Acidic

MOUTH FEEL / TANNINS

(REDS ONLY)

○ Very Smooth

○ A Little Rough Around the Edges

○ Makes Me Have to Lick My Chops

ALCOHOL

○ Not Noticeable

○ A Little Hot

○ Very Hot!

FINISH

○ Short   ○ Long

○ Medium   ○ Very Long

RATE IT !

★ ★ ★ ★ ★

50
Wine Tasting
Score Card

Wine Tasting Score Card

	# 1	# 2	# 3	# 4	# 5
Appearance					
Aroma					
Body					
Taste					
Finish					
Total					
Max	25	25	25	25	25
Label					

rank each category zero to five

Wine Tasting Score Card

	#1	#2	#3	#4	#5
Appearance					
Aroma					
Body					
Taste					
Finish					
Total					
Max	25	25	25	25	25
Label					

rank each category zero to five

Wine Tasting Score Card

	# 1	# 2	# 3	# 4	# 5
Appearance					
Aroma					
Body					
Taste					
Finish					
Total					
Max	25	25	25	25	25
Label					

rank each category zero to five

Wine Tasting Score Card

	#1	#2	#3	#4	#5
Appearance					
Aroma					
Body					
Taste					
Finish					

	#1	#2	#3	#4	#5
Total					
Max	25	25	25	25	25

Label					

rank each category zero to five

Wine Tasting Score Card

	#1	#2	#3	#4	#5
Appearance					
Aroma					
Body					
Taste					
Finish					
Total					
Max	25	25	25	25	25
Label					

rank each category zero to five

Wine Tasting Score Card

	#1	#2	#3	#4	#5
Appearance					
Aroma					
Body					
Taste					
Finish					
Total					
Max	25	25	25	25	25
Label					

rank each category zero to five

Wine Tasting Score Card

	# 1	# 2	# 3	# 4	# 5
Appearance					
Aroma					
Body					
Taste					
Finish					
Total					
Max	25	25	25	25	25
Label					

rank each category zero to five

Wine Tasting Score Card

	#1	#2	#3	#4	#5
Appearance					
Aroma					
Body					
Taste					
Finish					
Total					
Max	25	25	25	25	25
Label					

rank each category zero to five

Wine Tasting Score Card

	# 1	# 2	# 3	# 4	# 5
Appearance					
Aroma					
Body					
Taste					
Finish					
Total					
Max	25	25	25	25	25
Label					

rank each category zero to five

Wine Tasting Score Card

	# 1	# 2	# 3	# 4	# 5
Appearance					
Aroma					
Body					
Taste					
Finish					
Total					
Max	25	25	25	25	25
Label					

rank each category zero to five

Wine Tasting Score Card

	# 1	# 2	# 3	# 4	# 5
Appearance					
Aroma					
Body					
Taste					
Finish					

	# 1	# 2	# 3	# 4	# 5
Total					
Max	25	25	25	25	25

	# 1	# 2	# 3	# 4	# 5
Label					

rank each category zero to five

Wine Tasting Score Card

	# 1	# 2	# 3	# 4	# 5
Appearance					
Aroma					
Body					
Taste					
Finish					

	# 1	# 2	# 3	# 4	# 5
Total					
Max	25	25	25	25	25

	# 1	# 2	# 3	# 4	# 5
Label					

rank each category zero to five

Wine Tasting Score Card

	# 1	# 2	# 3	# 4	# 5
Appearance					
Aroma					
Body					
Taste					
Finish					
Total					
Max	25	25	25	25	25
Label					

rank each category zero to five

Wine Tasting Score Card

	# 1	# 2	# 3	# 4	# 5
Appearance					
Aroma					
Body					
Taste					
Finish					
Total					
Max	25	25	25	25	25
Label					

rank each category zero to five

Wine Tasting Score Card

	# 1	# 2	# 3	# 4	# 5
Appearance					
Aroma					
Body					
Taste					
Finish					
Total					
Max	25	25	25	25	25
Label					

rank each category zero to five

Wine Tasting Score Card

	#1	#2	#3	#4	#5
Appearance					
Aroma					
Body					
Taste					
Finish					

	#1	#2	#3	#4	#5
Total					
Max	25	25	25	25	25

	#1	#2	#3	#4	#5
Label					

rank each category zero to five

Wine Tasting Score Card

	# 1	# 2	# 3	# 4	# 5
Appearance					
Aroma					
Body					
Taste					
Finish					
Total					
Max	25	25	25	25	25
Label					

rank each category zero to five

Wine Tasting Score Card

	# 1	# 2	# 3	# 4	# 5
Appearance					
Aroma					
Body					
Taste					
Finish					
Total					
Max	25	25	25	25	25
Label					

rank each category zero to five

Wine Tasting Score Card

	# 1	# 2	# 3	# 4	# 5
Appearance					
Aroma					
Body					
Taste					
Finish					
Total					
Max	25	25	25	25	25
Label					

rank each category zero to five

Wine Tasting Score Card

	# 1	# 2	# 3	# 4	# 5
Appearance					
Aroma					
Body					
Taste					
Finish					
Total					
Max	25	25	25	25	25
Label					

rank each category zero to five

Wine Tasting Score Card

	# 1	# 2	# 3	# 4	# 5
Appearance					
Aroma					
Body					
Taste					
Finish					
Total					
Max	25	25	25	25	25
Label					

rank each category zero to five

Wine Tasting Score Card

	# 1	# 2	# 3	# 4	# 5
Appearance					
Aroma					
Body					
Taste					
Finish					
Total					
Max	25	25	25	25	25
Label					

rank each category zero to five

Wine Tasting Score Card

	# 1	# 2	# 3	# 4	# 5
Appearance					
Aroma					
Body					
Taste					
Finish					

	# 1	# 2	# 3	# 4	# 5
Total					
Max	25	25	25	25	25

	# 1	# 2	# 3	# 4	# 5
Label					

rank each category zero to five

Wine Tasting Score Card

	# 1	# 2	# 3	# 4	# 5
Appearance					
Aroma					
Body					
Taste					
Finish					
Total					
Max	25	25	25	25	25
Label					

rank each category zero to five

Wine Tasting Score Card

	#1	#2	#3	#4	#5
Appearance					
Aroma					
Body					
Taste					
Finish					

	#1	#2	#3	#4	#5
Total					
Max	25	25	25	25	25

	#1	#2	#3	#4	#5
Label					

rank each category zero to five

Wine Tasting Score Card

	# 1	# 2	# 3	# 4	# 5
Appearance					
Aroma					
Body					
Taste					
Finish					
Total					
Max	25	25	25	25	25
Label					

rank each category zero to five

Wine Tasting Score Card

	# 1	# 2	# 3	# 4	# 5
Appearance					
Aroma					
Body					
Taste					
Finish					

	# 1	# 2	# 3	# 4	# 5
Total					
Max	25	25	25	25	25

	# 1	# 2	# 3	# 4	# 5
Label					

rank each category zero to five

Wine Tasting Score Card

	#1	#2	#3	#4	#5
Appearance					
Aroma					
Body					
Taste					
Finish					
Total					
Max	25	25	25	25	25
Label					

rank each category zero to five

Wine Tasting Score Card

	# 1	# 2	# 3	# 4	# 5
Appearance					
Aroma					
Body					
Taste					
Finish					

	# 1	# 2	# 3	# 4	# 5
Total					
Max	25	25	25	25	25

Label					

rank each category zero to five

Wine Tasting Score Card

	#1	#2	#3	#4	#5
Appearance					
Aroma					
Body					
Taste					
Finish					

	#1	#2	#3	#4	#5
Total					
Max	25	25	25	25	25

	#1	#2	#3	#4	#5
Label					

rank each category zero to five

Wine Tasting Score Card

	# 1	# 2	# 3	# 4	# 5
Appearance					
Aroma					
Body					
Taste					
Finish					
Total					
Max	25	25	25	25	25
Label					

rank each category zero to five

Wine Tasting Score Card

	# 1	# 2	# 3	# 4	# 5
Appearance					
Aroma					
Body					
Taste					
Finish					
Total					
Max	25	25	25	25	25
Label					

rank each category zero to five

Wine Tasting Score Card

	# 1	# 2	# 3	# 4	# 5
Appearance					
Aroma					
Body					
Taste					
Finish					
Total					
Max	25	25	25	25	25
Label					

rank each category zero to five

Wine Tasting Score Card

	# 1	# 2	# 3	# 4	# 5
Appearance					
Aroma					
Body					
Taste					
Finish					

	# 1	# 2	# 3	# 4	# 5
Total					
Max	25	25	25	25	25

	# 1	# 2	# 3	# 4	# 5
Label					

rank each category zero to five

Wine Tasting Score Card

	# 1	# 2	# 3	# 4	# 5
Appearance					
Aroma					
Body					
Taste					
Finish					
Total					
Max	25	25	25	25	25
Label					

rank each category zero to five

Wine Tasting Score Card

	#1	#2	#3	#4	#5
Appearance					
Aroma					
Body					
Taste					
Finish					
Total					
Max	25	25	25	25	25
Label					

rank each category zero to five

Wine Tasting Score Card

	#1	#2	#3	#4	#5
Appearance					
Aroma					
Body					
Taste					
Finish					
Total					
Max	25	25	25	25	25
Label					

rank each category zero to five

Wine Tasting Score Card

	# 1	# 2	# 3	# 4	# 5
Appearance					
Aroma					
Body					
Taste					
Finish					

	# 1	# 2	# 3	# 4	# 5
Total					
Max	25	25	25	25	25

Label					

rank each category zero to five

Wine Tasting Score Card

	# 1	# 2	# 3	# 4	# 5
Appearance					
Aroma					
Body					
Taste					
Finish					

	# 1	# 2	# 3	# 4	# 5
Total					
Max	25	25	25	25	25

	# 1	# 2	# 3	# 4	# 5
Label					

rank each category zero to five

Wine Tasting Score Card

	#1	#2	#3	#4	#5
Appearance					
Aroma					
Body					
Taste					
Finish					

	#1	#2	#3	#4	#5
Total					
Max	25	25	25	25	25

	#1	#2	#3	#4	#5
Label					

rank each category zero to five

Wine Tasting Score Card

	# 1	# 2	# 3	# 4	# 5
Appearance					
Aroma					
Body					
Taste					
Finish					

	# 1	# 2	# 3	# 4	# 5
Total					
Max	25	25	25	25	25

	# 1	# 2	# 3	# 4	# 5
Label					

rank each category zero to five

Wine Tasting Score Card

	#1	#2	#3	#4	#5
Appearance					
Aroma					
Body					
Taste					
Finish					

	#1	#2	#3	#4	#5
Total					
Max	25	25	25	25	25

Label				

rank each category zero to five

Wine Tasting Score Card

	# 1	# 2	# 3	# 4	# 5
Appearance					
Aroma					
Body					
Taste					
Finish					
Total					
Max	25	25	25	25	25
Label					

rank each category zero to five

Wine Tasting Score Card

	#1	#2	#3	#4	#5
Appearance					
Aroma					
Body					
Taste					
Finish					

	#1	#2	#3	#4	#5
Total					
Max	25	25	25	25	25

	#1	#2	#3	#4	#5
Label					

rank each category zero to five

Wine Tasting Score Card

	# 1	# 2	# 3	# 4	# 5
Appearance					
Aroma					
Body					
Taste					
Finish					
Total					
Max	25	25	25	25	25
Label					

rank each category zero to five

Wine Tasting Score Card

	# 1	# 2	# 3	# 4	# 5
Appearance					
Aroma					
Body					
Taste					
Finish					
Total					
Max	25	25	25	25	25
Label					

rank each category zero to five

Wine Tasting Score Card

	# 1	# 2	# 3	# 4	# 5
Appearance					
Aroma					
Body					
Taste					
Finish					

	# 1	# 2	# 3	# 4	# 5
Total					
Max	25	25	25	25	25

	# 1	# 2	# 3	# 4	# 5
Label					

rank each category zero to five

Wine Tasting Score Card

	# 1	# 2	# 3	# 4	# 5
Appearance					
Aroma					
Body					
Taste					
Finish					
Total					
Max	25	25	25	25	25
Label					

rank each category zero to five

Wine Tasting Score Card

	# 1	# 2	# 3	# 4	# 5
Appearance					
Aroma					
Body					
Taste					
Finish					
Total					
Max	25	25	25	25	25
Label					

rank each category zero to five

Wine Tasting Score Card

	# 1	# 2	# 3	# 4	# 5
Appearance					
Aroma					
Body					
Taste					
Finish					

	# 1	# 2	# 3	# 4	# 5
Total					
Max	25	25	25	25	25

Label					

rank each category zero to five